DATA STRATEGY

SELLING THE VALUE

Dr. Doug McConchie

DEDICATION

To my father, Roy Pymble McConchie

Published by Dr. Doug McConchie, 2021
ISBN: 9798509954023
All rights reserved.

ACKNOWLEDGEMENTS

When deciding to write this book the world was in the midst of Covid restrictions. It was an extraordinary time, hopefully not to be repeated. But if there was one positive that came true as a result of those events, it was that the lack of mobility to venture outside did mean that taking my time to sit at the kitchen table in front of the computer screen and type these words was a realistic possibility. In more normal times there are so many other distractions!

Even so, I must offer my thanks to Mindy Gibbins-Klein for sharing her experience and offering her structured advice and support in encouraging my writing. Without her guidance my learning curve would have been so much longer. Through the writing process, I have come to learn that a book is not a solo activity and writing this book is no exception. Please can I take this opportunity to sincerely thank my reviewers for taking time out of their own busy lives to read and improve this work. In no particular order: Daniel Nisser at Outokumpu, David Wilson at ISS, Greg Buckle at EDF Energy, Matt Tolhurst at UCAS, Alex Lewis at Schroders, Phil Gibbins-Klein at Queenswood School and Julian Ford at INTO. Your feedback really was helpful and gave me the confidence that there was someone out there who might find a book on Data Strategy – Selling the Value useful!

Many thanks too go to Alison Turner for her dedication to reading every word and editing this work. Likewise, Edward Trayer: a big thank you for helping me turn this book into reality at Amazon and beyond.

Finally and perhaps foremost, thank you Ludovic for allowing me to take over the kitchen table and put pen to paper in the first place.

CONTENTS

INTRODUCTION 1

CHAPTER 1: Selling Value is creative, dynamic and entrepreneurial .. 12
- Data Strategy is creative 13
- Data Strategy is dynamic 14
- Data Strategy is entrepreneurial 15
- Proof of Value / Concept 16
- Selling Value Communications 17
- Case Study: Securing buy-in to building Data Strategy value in a leading Insurer 19

CHAPTER 2: Know your audience 23
- C-suite Executives 23
- Data Users 24
- Data Processors 25
- Data Owners and Data Stewards 26
- Resistance 26
- What is the value of Data Strategy? 28
- Case Study: Targeted value communications in the Utility Sector ... 29

CHAPTER 3: Understand your level of data maturity 31
- What is data maturity? 31
- The practicalities of data maturity assessment delivery 34
- Building a Roadmap to improvement 35
- Roadmap progress measurement 38
- Case Study: Building Data Maturity in the Airline industry 39

CHAPTER 4: Implement Technology but not just for Technology's sake 41
- Use technology to drive value 41
- Technology costs more than the initial purchase price 43
- Focus on core principals 44
- Remember that new technology is accompanied by new ways of working 45
- How to quantify the value of Technology related activities 47
- Security needs to be considered throughout Technology related activities 48
- Case Study: A data platform fiasco in the Fast-Moving Consumer Goods sector 49

CHAPTER 5: Think People 51
  Be realistic about people capabilities 51
  Data roles and responsibilities 53
  Be ambitious with your people, but avoid pitfalls 54
  Target Operating Model 57
  How to quantify the value of People related activities? 58
  Security needs to be considered throughout People related
  activities 59
  Case Study: Best practice organisational structures in Banking 60

CHAPTER 6: Finding the right level of Governance 63
  Governance of your Data Strategy itself 64
  Governance of your data related activities 64
  Governance enables and requires effective communication 69
  How to quantify the value of Governance related activities 69
  Security needs to be considered throughout Governance related
  activities 70
  Case Study: Governance in the Nuclear sector 71

CHAPTER 7: Adapt processes to work well in your organisation 73
  Review your existing data related processes 73
  Roles and responsibilities in data related processes 75
  No-people processes 75
  Data etiquette 76
  Process typology 77
  How to quantify the value of Process related activities? 78
  Security needs to be considered throughout Process related
  activities 80
  Case Study: Evidence based Manufacturing process management .. 81

CHAPTER 8: You must deliver incrementally 83
  Incremental Value Add 83
  Foundational activities 85
  Data Strategy evolves 87
  Data Strategy should still be partly radical 88
  Case Study: Customer facing solution development in the Road
  Transport Sector 89

CHAPTER 9: Data is the untapped asset in your organisation 91
  Strategic intent is needed 93
  Growing recognition for data as an asset 93
  How to quantify the value of Data related activities 95
  Security needs to be considered throughout Data related activities 98

Case Study: Building new data driven business propositions in Insurance 98
CHAPTER 10: Some data is better than others 101
　Data typology 101
　Data capture 102
　Data storage 103
　Data cleaning 105
　Data monetisation 106
　Mission critical data 107
　Case Study: Data in the world of Healthcare 107
CONCLUSION 110

TABLE OF FIGURES

Figure 1: The Data Strategy Framework 7
Figure 2: Example Three Year Roadmap 22
Figure 3: Communications Plan Template 28
Figure 4: From information to optimisation through improved data analytics maturity 33
Figure 5: Example Data Strategy Roadmap by Delivery Theme 37
Figure 6: The Continuous Improvement Cycle 68
Figure 7: Example Business Case Template 85
Figure 8: Data Strategy Implementation 94
Figure 9: A centralised and localised Business Intelligence & Analytics delivery model 97

INTRODUCTION

Data is everywhere. Data is building-up around us in ever increasing volumes. Almost everything we do in our personal and professional lives now leaves a digital trail and, as a result, data volumes are growing exponentially. To describe the scale of the increase in data, according to the Information Overload Resource Group, in the past two years alone 90% of the world's total data has been created. This statistic of incredible growth in data demonstrates the need for organisations to urgently address their data management and, if they are not already doing so, to take their data seriously as the important asset it is. If organisations don't act now, their data estates risk to grow chaotically and become even more difficult to manage. Other assets like People and Finance have had whole departments looking after them for decades, but for far too long data, has been left alone and not managed as effectively as it could be.

This statistic needs to also be seen as a call to arms to turn data into value: new insights, new business propositions, new tools and new applications can be built from this expanding ocean of data. So many exciting things are happening today with data, it's time for all organisations to embrace the opportunities available from using data to deliver value. The fact that data can be used in so many different ways to do so many different things, is why a Data Strategy is needed to help navigate the choices about what is best for your organisation in how it uses data and how it can generate value from the data it uses.

A Data Strategy needs to align to 'Corporate' or 'Organisational' Strategy: its Mission and Purpose. The Data Strategy is the description of how data needs to be consumed, managed and exploited to achieve the organisation's strategy and how the data related activities across the organisation support the organisation's mission and purpose. Data Strategy and Organisational Strategy are fundamentally joined with the successful delivery of Data Strategy being an enabler of the successful implementation of Organisational Strategy. A Data Strategy must not be developed in isolation and needs to be maintained in conjunction with Organisational Strategy. When an Organisational Strategy evolves and is refocused, so too will the Data Strategy need to be checked to ensure its continued alignment.

DATA STRATEGY – SELLING THE VALUE

Data is so intrinsic to all activities in an organisation, isolating thought processes about data from other organisational activities can become difficult. It is because data is used across the entire organisation and is so fundamental to what all parts of the organisation does, that a Data Strategy is needed to manage it effectively and efficiently for all parts of the organisation. Without having this, what may work well for one area of the organisation, may be a disaster elsewhere.

Some organisations are undergoing a Digital Transformation process and this requires a massive effort to use data effectively. Other organisations will be pursuing 'exciting' growth strategies or mergers and acquisitions or cost cutting exercises or R&D drives, etc. In all cases, while these strategic activities are being pursued, other parts of the organisation will be conducting the relatively more 'mundane' business-as-usual work, for example, around Administrative processes, Supply, Invoicing, Regulatory Reporting, Health & Safety, Building Maintenance, Support Services, etc. The use of data across all of these activity areas needs to be brought together coherently and be carefully managed so that data is available to support the successful delivery of their work. A Data Strategy needs to support both the exciting and the more mundane.

Each data source is a discrete set of information with its own intrinsic value, but also it can be combined with other data sets to provide even more additional value. The more data that is used and combined however, the more complex it is to manage and the greater the need to think strategically about its use. Increasingly organisations are using a wide mix of data in new ways to drive new business opportunities. To give just a few examples, recent times have seen an explosion of digital e-commerce channels across the internet to replace or work alongside traditional face-to-face market interactions, new collaboration tools are also transforming the way people interact with customers, suppliers and colleagues in their workplaces and a whole series of internet linked smart-devices have been marketed to make our lives easier both at work and at home. Each of these initiatives relies on bringing data together from a variety of sources and building out innovative data solutions. Managing data processes across these initiatives needs to be carefully thought through and ultimately needs to sit within the context of the organisation's Data Strategy.

At the extreme, some organisations are going through a complete digitalisation metamorphosis: literally rethinking their existing ways of working, removing manual intervention and automating their operational flows end-to-end through the use of data. These digital factories, digital hospitals and digital airlines, to again name but a few, have started on an on-going mission to transform their existing activities making them more efficient and effective, more competitive and successful, through the use of data. Having a robust Data Strategy here will be essential if the digitalisation is to be successful.

In many places, however, data is also an untapped raw resource yet to be handled in any way. Stores of data have been built up in many organisations awaiting a use case and waiting to be used. These untapped data sets sit in their various formats, with differing levels of quality and unquantified value. Not until a specific use case is found can the true value or the appropriate handling processes be defined, including data cleaning and preparation processes to make the data more valuable. A Data Strategy is needed to consider all data sources and how they should be managed during their lifecycle.

This book examines the variety of data and the full lifecycle of its use. We explore some of the different types of data and its potential to gain value. In so doing, we think about the transformation journey of data from end-to-end: how it is currently being handled en-route to being consumed in the many potential use cases and how it should be handled in the future. The book also explores data capture and ingestion. We look at data processing including the importance of data architecture, modelling, governance and security. We look at the role of technology in the use of data. And, we emphasise the importance of building value-adding outputs, including Analytics, Applications and Business Intelligence solutions.

When exploring this transformation journey, we also look at the ways of working when handling data and the different delivery methodologies in use from Waterfall to Agile and DevOps to DataOps. We examine some of the process re-engineering practices that can be applied, drawing on Lean thinking and process optimisation best practices. We also examine how these impact on the data etiquette within the organisation and support the building of a successful data culture.

All of the above data related activities are implemented in different ways in different organisations. How they are put together needs to be right for the organisation's individual circumstances. To bring these together: all organisations today need to have a Data Strategy in place that provides guidance to staff and other stakeholders on what is its approach and vision for the use of data. Each organisation's Data Strategy is unique, reflecting their specific data sets, their existing technology and architecture, their people skills and capabilities as well as the different ways of working and processes that are deployed in that organisation. The Data Strategy not only reflects what the current situation within the organisation related to data and its data related activities, but it also positions the organisation in the best way to respond to its future needs.

This book cannot cover all aspects involved with Data Strategy in every detail. Instead, it will aim to highlight some of the important questions and areas that need to be examined and leaves the reader to drill-down on specific topics in further detail elsewhere. It draws on my experience of having worked in Consulting and having provided advisory support and services to a wide range of public and private sector organisations, helping these customers to pursue their data related initiatives. It also shares some of the lessons learned from having set-up a Data Strategy Consulting Practice and having learned how best to secure the commitment of customers to implement their Data Strategy.

The primary audience for Data Strategy – *Selling the Value* is those readers working in medium to large organisations considering their next data related actions in a fairly complex and sophisticated data environment. The reader may be about to make an initial start on defining their Data Strategy or they may be considering why some of their data related activities are not achieving the success they had hoped. They may be searching for guidance on how to extract more return from their data investments or looking for help on how to de-risk some of their data related activities. The reader has probably spent many years working in technology, so does not need this book to expand on the merits of certain technologies versus others, but while it is assumed the reader has some knowledge on most topics covered, they probably have not developed any or certainly not many Data Strategies. So, this book will focus on the key topics and themes to be looked at across Data Strategy to better assess the current state of performance in an organisation's data related activities and how to best define the next level of performance in those areas.

I hope too though, that this book is accessible to all readers interested in data. I have on purpose written the content in a way that guides readers of all backgrounds through the essential elements they should consider when using data and carrying-out data related activities. In reality, multiple books can be written on each and every aspect of these elements. Instead, these pages are designed to describe the high-level considerations needed to enable the successful use of data and they point the reader toward the elements that they decide need more detailed examination.

It is also worth noting at this point that throughout the book, reference is made to both business and public sector organisations. The terms are used interchangeably and any comments made are certainly applicable to both, as well as other tertiary sectors. For example, comments related to business benefits can be assumed to also include benefits to organisations of all types.

A Data Strategy is a written document that can be read and referred to by relevant parties, that outlines the journey from where an organisation is today in its use of data to where it wants to be in the future. The component parts of a Data Strategy include:

1) an impartial assessment setting out the current state of data and data related activities within the organisation,
2) building on this assessment, a clear articulation of what in the future the data and data related activities need to be, including a long-term Vision,
3) a Roadmap and supporting Business Case for the initiatives within the Roadmap identifying the sequence and timelines for implementation, as well as the value to be delivered,
4) a Target Operating Model for the organisation needed to enable successful delivery and governance of data and data related activities, including the Roadmap, Data Architecture and Technology Inventory, and
5) a list of stakeholders impacted by the Data Strategy and a Communications Plan identifying how they will be informed.

To help frame our thinking around Data Strategy, we use as our reference a tried and tested approach that has been fine-tuned over the years of my Consulting work and that helps ensure the organisation is looked at holistically but also in the necessary detail to make a robust assessment of its Data Strategy needs. As shown in Figure 1 below, the framework is used to examine the organisation from different perspectives and assess its capabilities from these perspectives. In every organisation there will be some strengths in the capabilities the organisation already has that will need to be continued and built on, but there will also be some gaps and weaknesses that will need to be filled or improved. The assessment of capabilities needs to be made in an appropriate context. That context is the degree the capabilities support the delivery of value and organisational Strategy today. As well as, how well those capabilities equip the organisation to deliver successfully in the future. For example, in simplistic terms, if a business strategy is to become a market leader, the supporting Data Strategy needs to set out how its data related activities will enable the business in its ambitions.

We focus in this book on a key aspect: the need to sell the value of a Data Strategy. This focus is often overlooked and the importance is under-estimated by those defining and implementing a Data Strategy. By forgetting the importance of *Selling the Value* of Data Strategy however, the risk is a Data Strategy is not successfully delivered. A Data Strategy that does not include a Roadmap and supporting Business Case, is really only a document outlining a series of dreams. It is easy to dream of a future that is not constrained by any reality: unlimited financial resources, infinite staffing capabilities, technologies that work right first time, datasets that have perfect quality, etc. Unfortunately, this is never the real case and choices, preferences and priorities have to be made. The Roadmap and Business Case force the reality to be captured on to paper. *Selling the Value* is the wording that underpins this reality. It reminds the authors of Data Strategy to clearly articulate upfront, during and at the end of implementation the importance of the Data Strategy and to communicate the benefits anticipated as well as delivered.

If an adequate Business Case for an item on the Roadmap cannot be made, then this is a strong hint to reconsider its inclusion. If senior stakeholders cannot buy-in to the Data Strategy Roadmap and fully support its deployment, then it will unlikely receive the commitment it needs to make its implementation a success.

Figure 1: The Data Strategy Framework

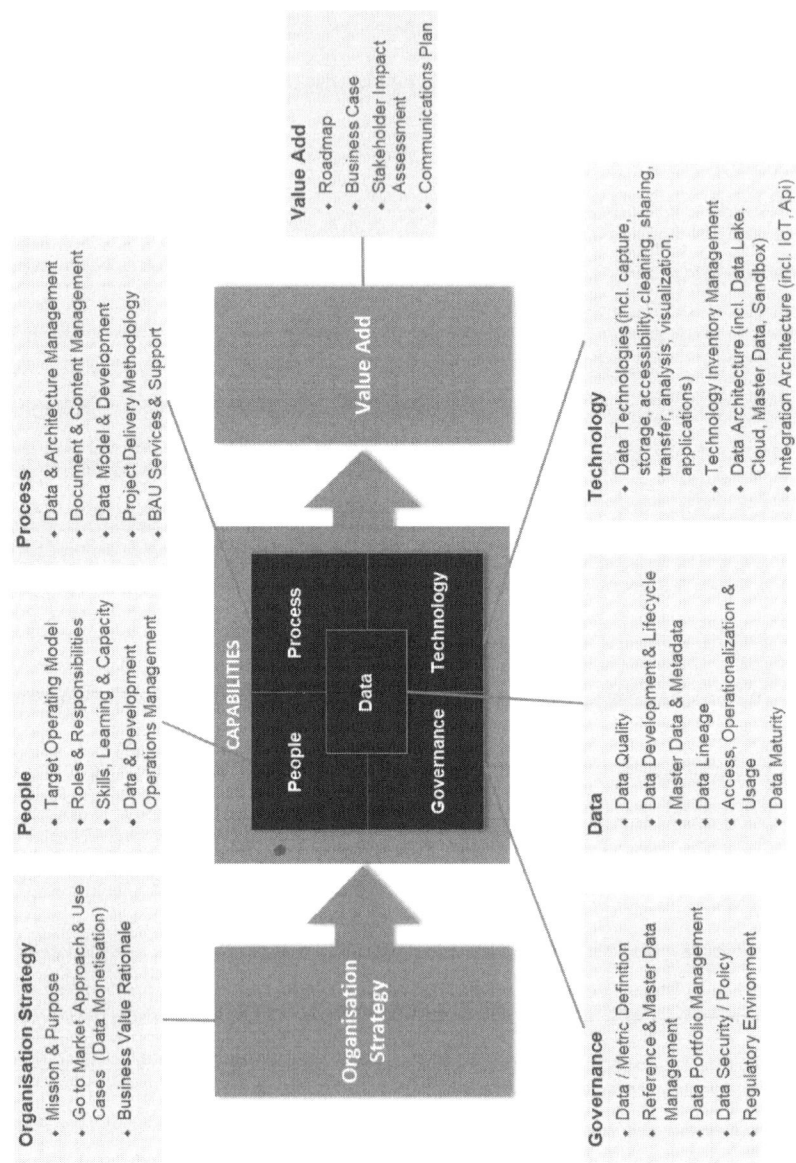

If an initiative on the Roadmap fails to deliver the anticipated benefits, at the very least lessons should be learned about what occurred so similar events do not re-occur in the future. If an initiative on the Roadmap does deliver, stakeholders should certainly be informed about this success, helping build confidence in the rest of the Data Strategy and celebrate the benefits gained from the delivery of this part of the Data Strategy Roadmap. Too often Data Strategies are defined and shelved as interesting documents not to be looked at again. They should not be. A Data Strategy is a living document needing to be kept up-to-date and frequently communicated. *Selling the Value* of Data Strategy ensures commitment from all involved and this commitment makes the chances of successful delivery so much higher.

A Data Strategy needs to be delivered using a clear and robust framework that enables aspirations to be commonly agreed, subsequent implementation plans to be rigorously defined and delivery to be successfully achieved. Without following a structured approach to *Selling the Value* to stakeholders, the Data Strategy risks lacking stakeholder buy-in to the Data Strategy initiatives. And, without commitment to the initiatives, stakeholders are unlikely to support the delivery of the wider Roadmap. Regardless of how good the Data Strategy is and how valuable the Data Strategy will be for the organisation, unfortunately, a Roadmap that does not receive the buy-in and commitment of stakeholders means the Data Strategy delivery will likely not be successfully achieved. Just as, a Data Strategy that is not robust or is missing some of the key elements needed, is unlikely to succeed.

In this book, I set out how to enable successful Data Strategy and we examine each of the elements needed. In Chapter 1, we build on why selling value is important. We examine why Data Strategy needs to be written in a creative, dynamic and entrepreneurial way. Ultimately the Data Strategy document needs to engage the reader and secure their buy-in to the Roadmap delivery. To support this, we outline how a Proof of Value and / or Concept can be used to test and demonstrate delivery success. We also examine the need to develop a Communications plan for stakeholders to maintain their engagement levels and keep them informed of progress.

In Chapter 2, we focus on the refining the right message for the right audience. *Selling the Value* of Data Strategy is like any other sales messaging: it should be targeted to audience needs. We look at the needs of some key stakeholders involved in the delivery of any Data Strategy and we examine how to work at securing greater buy-in and overcoming resistance by maintaining a laser-focus on the value add delivered by the Data Strategy.

In Chapter 3, we look at how to conduct a current state assessment of data maturity. This assessment is the starting point and basis for future Data Strategy development, so we discuss some of the important practicalities around conducting these assessments. A key practicality is deciding on which areas to prioritise for improvement and so we discuss some of the different options to consider in building a Data Strategy Roadmap, including establishing the Business Case for the different data related activities. We also examine how this Business Case comes with a timeframe and set of project milestones to be delivered against.

In Chapter 4, we return to the Data Strategy Framework and take a specific look at Technology and its part within a Data Strategy. We emphasise technology is deployed to drive value, so when considering the deployment of new technology, we need to consider the cost-benefit analysis of technology choices. We think about the full range of costs that will be incurred during its implementation lifecycle and balance these against the true value add benefits delivered from the deployment of that new technology.

In Chapter 5, we examine the People aspect of the Data Strategy Framework. We recognise Data Strategy is implemented by people for people and so the need to improve capabilities for data related staff and data literacy across all stakeholders is discussed. Some of the options around staffing data related activists are reviewed, as are the roles and responsibilities of key team members involved in the definition and delivery of the Data Strategy. We also examine how People costs and savings are typically quantified in Data Strategy initiatives.

In Chapter 6, we review another key aspect of the Data Strategy Framework: Governance practices. Here we look at the need to find an appropriate balance between too much and too little governance. We firstly examine how to govern the Data Strategy itself and then move on to wider governance practices that will be needed during Roadmap implementation and business-as-usual operation of data related activities. We also examine the communication and security aspects of governance practices.

In Chapter 7, we focus on the Process aspect of the Data Strategy Framework. Here we examine how to better align existing processes and adopt new processes to support the delivery of the Data Strategy. We start with looking at the importance of defining the roles and responsibilities of staff involved in processes. We then examine processes that do not involve people. Returning to ways of working, we discuss the need to develop a data etiquette among staff and how the choice of different delivery methodologies, including Agile, DevOps and DataOps, will impact this. We also review how process improvements can be best quantified for inclusion in Data Strategy Business Cases.

In Chapter 8, we bring together our recommendations to deliver a Data Strategy incrementally and how this incremental value add is best described in the Data Strategy Roadmap. And, we think about incremental value add from a Lean perspective, from an evolutionary or continuous improvement perspective and from a radical change perspective.

In Chapter 9, we come back to the Data Strategy Framework and look at the Data aspect. We examine how data is the untapped asset in an organisation and how organisations of all types are transforming to secure the benefits of data driven change. We identify what is the Data Strategy implementation process, focusing on the need for strategic intent to be defined in order for its implementation to be successfully managed. We also discuss the growing recognition among organisations for data as an asset, examining how data and data related initiatives are typically quantified in Data Strategy Business Cases.

In Chapter 10, we continue our examination of Data, reminding readers of the various sources and types of data. We then follow the data lifecycle from raw data, through storage, cleaning to its monetisation and consumption. We focus also on the importance of managing Mission Critical Data effectively.

Through these 10 Chapters, I have endeavoured to make the case on why *Selling the Value* of Data Strategy is important to enabling its successful delivery, securing the buy-in of stakeholders and helping prioritise and manage the difficult choices in identifying and delivering the Roadmap. At the end of each Chapter a short Case Study is provided to illustrate from the real world how organisations have addressed some of the key questions identified in that Chapter. And, through these pages, this book sets out what is needed for successful Data Strategy development and how, with a robust Data Strategy in place and worked toward, your organisation will be better placed to secure the important benefits that data can bring.

CHAPTER 1: Selling Value is creative, dynamic and entrepreneurial

Data Strategy so often starts at the point of failure and disappointment. Perhaps a technology implementation has failed to deliver or some mission critical data has been found to have significant errors or time to insight is simply just taking too long compared to competitors. Regardless of the reason, a crunch time has arrived and the organisation realises that a step change is needed. Over the years, many clients have approached me asking for assistance to turnaround their lack lustre progress in extracting value from their data. Clients have recounted the fact that they have spent many months and sadly sometimes multiple millions in rolling-out data initiatives in their organisations that have failed to deliver on their promise. They ask how can we turn this around and how do we start afresh?

My first response is to reassure them. They are not alone! Many organisations struggle to achieve the success they initially desired from data related programmes. It is a common problem, but the good news is that it is also a problem that can be solved. And, the benefits from getting the improvements in place are huge!

The reasons for disappointment can be many and it can be helpful to review the lessons learned from past attempts, but over and above the specific individual learnings of each case, the important thing to remember is to learn from the past and move forward positively. Failed initiatives in the past provide valuable learnings on how not to do it the future: Rome was not built in a day!

Other clients may have had successes in their individual data initiatives and have useful Case Studies of their pioneering projects to share. Great news! These isolated achievements however typically fail to deliver a coordinated and systemic approach that can be leveraged for the next data initiative. One-off use cases are helpful, but they are not a fully-fledged Data Strategy. The important point though is, not to diminish past successes or wring hands over past failures, instead it is to recognise that the time is now right to build a robust Data Strategy and focus on *Selling the Value* that its implementation will bring.

Data Strategy is creative

Data Strategy needs to be written in a way that captures the hearts and minds of all those in the organisation. It needs to have sufficient detail and content that resonates and delivers value for all stakeholders. It needs to outline the aspirations and vision for organisational data initiatives. It also needs to spell out the practical intermediate steps from short term, through the medium term and into the long term for data related activities.

Key to describing a Data Strategy is the articulation of the benefits that stakeholders will achieve from its successful implementation. These benefits need to be targeted to the stakeholder groups within the organisation. Describing the value that will be created from data is at the core of successful Data Strategy.

Data Strategy needs to be aligned to Business or Organisational Strategy. The Business Strategy, Mission and or Purpose sets out the overarching objectives for the organisation and Data Strategy needs to be defined in a way to support the successful delivery of these. In doing so, there are a wide range of creative initiatives that can be pursued.

Creativity is needed in delivering value: existing solutions will need to be improved overtime and new solutions are needed to enhance existing data initiatives and develop new areas of value. Creative solutions provide the opportunity to learn and improve organisational data capabilities. Some creativity will undoubtedly fail or at least not be as successful as hoped, but these failings in turn provide opportunities for learning about what not to do. Finding the right mix of truly innovative and more tried and tested approaches is needed, but the need to integrate creativity into any Data Strategy will pay dividends.

Innovation within the Data Strategy can be in many forms, ranging from radically new data driven business propositions to new ways of operation to better handle data and everywhere in between. For example, a Pizza business developed a new business channel as part of its Data Strategy. It extended its e-commerce store to include Alexa and Siri voice activation. Now its customers can verbally build their pizza, selecting favourite toppings and choosing preferred drinks all through a structured 'voice recognised' Artificial Intelligence based conversation with their mobile virtual assistant. Elsewhere, the introduction of a Data Dictionary in another retailer's business brought enormous benefits by simply better managing the commonly used nomenclature across the organisation: speeding up internal processes by having standard definitions for key data, introducing a governed approach to updating master data and enabling stakeholders to start building greater trust in its evidence-based insights. The limit to data driven creativity is literally the imagination itself!

Data Strategy is dynamic

Data sets are changing all the time. New data arrives from existing systems and new data sets are identified from new sources. New technical or process related solutions are continuously being introduced offering new capabilities and ways of working that have not previously been available. This dynamism provides a heartbeat to data programmes. The changing environment stimulates data related work and provides a driver for change.

A fully developed Data Strategy contains short-term deliverables: covering quick wins, initial pilots and early-stage outputs that are the foundations on which future developments are built. These initial deliverables are demonstrations of the value that could be achieved in the Data Strategy and how it will deliver pioneering benefits to the organisation across people, data, processes, technology and governance capabilities.

Over the medium to longer term, the capabilities an organisation starts with need to be further developed and refined. The scale and pace of change can be grown as confidence in delivery is achieved.

Agile Delivery methodologies play well in the Data Strategy space. They provide a programmatic set of outcomes throughout the delivery journey. While a Waterfall delivery methodology undoubtedly works and delivers Big Bang impact, increasingly stakeholders have come to realise the benefit of smaller and more regular drops throughout the delivery process. Agile tends to enable greater confidence that outcomes will be achieved, provides down payments of value to be made along the Data

Strategy journey and also allows for any necessary course corrections to be made early.

The need for continual improvement and dynamic responses to changing data and the data related environment are strong: we have all seen what happened to Kodak and Blockbuster when they tried to remain with physical film rather than embrace the digital age and we have all seen the impact of Airbnb or Wikipedia or Uber excelling in their digital domains. Standing still is not a viable option!

Over the years, I have unfortunately seen that it is all too easy to get stuck in planning mode and not make a start on the implementation of the Data Strategy. Organisations today should not expend all their energies on over-thinking their Roadmap, but instead focus on the near-horizon gains they wish to secure. Organisations do need to do sufficient definition work to identify and prioritise their initiatives, but they also need to quickly move on to the detailed design of their solutions and start building them as soon as possible. To help keep momentum, they should consider starting small and de-risking the delivery of initiatives, perhaps, as we will see below, by starting with a Proof of Concept to test solution viability. A dynamic approach is best to secure the benefits of data driven change: learning from implementing data initiatives is better than just thinking about them!

Data Strategy is entrepreneurial

All forward looking plans need to have a clear description of the benefits and costs involved. And, you don't need to be an entrepreneur to understand that the sum of the benefits needs to be greater than the sum of the costs. All of the proposed initiatives and improvements need to be incorporated into a Data Strategy Roadmap and each initiative needs a supporting Business Case.

The investment side of data initiatives is usually the easiest to define: it covers the cost of data ingestion, storage, transformation, transmission, security, visualisation and consumption. In the calculation of these costs, it is important to not only capture the upfront costs, but also estimates of the business-as-usual running costs and eventual decommissioning.

The returns from data initiatives can prove more difficult to define. When thinking about likely returns it is often helpful to consider these from different time perspectives, i.e., what new benefits will the deliverable generate that were not possible to achieve in the past? What are the benefits today from its delivery and what will they be going forward? Where possible, a good starting point in considering candidate Data Strategy initiatives is to consider their alignment to the business go-to-market approach: do these initiatives help secure improved customer value?

The value created might be the identification and/or generation of new insights, new processes and new capabilities. Alternatively, value may be generated from improving existing practices and/or making these more efficient. Here these efficiencies can helpfully be quantified to deliver estimated order of magnitude savings. Sometimes whole new business models can be developed, with the accompanying business case for their introduction being possible to define.

Being able to demonstrate where the Data Strategy has delivered value also helps in securing buy-in to scaling out similar data initiatives elsewhere. This multiplier effect – learn it once, repeat it many times – delivers compound returns on investment. This is something successful entrepreneurs know best.

Proof of Value / Concept

To better understand the value that a data initiative will bring, it is often helpful to start with an initial small-scale deployment that once proved successful can be rolled-out further. For example, if a manufacturing business conducted a proof of value (POV) exercise showing how the automated capture of data from a single piece of production line machinery would deliver significant levels of efficiency savings, then scaling out similar data automation processes across the whole production line is hopefully a good indication that similar benefits are scalable.

A proof of concept (POC) provides a similar opportunity to test the merits of a deployment in a small way before moving out to a full-scale implementation. For example, when looking to deploy a new data platform, testing a thin end-to-end slice of the chosen technologies allows for its suitability to be tested, different choices to be evaluated and a better more robust data platform architecture to be defined. Once the POC has been tested a full-scale deployment can follow with all the necessary test, development, pre-production, production and run environments being set-up.

Proofs of value / concept help validate concepts and ideas and by so doing help build confidence among stakeholders that any proposed Data Strategy initiatives are robust. They allow for learnings to be collected and acted on before too significant an investment or commitment is made. They should also allow for the subsequent real-scale deployments to be implemented in a faster manner. The chances of success of these real-scale deployments should also be greater having been de-risked through taking on-board the proof of value / concept learnings.

In one client organisation, when looking to gain savings from the implementation of a real-time stock taking application in a well-known Restaurant chain, a combined POC / POV was first undertaken to test the technology approach as well as to check that the identified savings could be generated. In fact, while the POC turned out to identify greater costs than initially anticipated, the POV also identified greater benefits from not just waste management cost savings, but also the improved returns generated from now being able to co-ordinate the running of restaurant specific promotional campaigns that used targeted stocks. Thanks to these POC/POV activities, the restaurant gained enough confidence to move ahead. They built-up a better understanding of the costs and returns from the subsequent implementation.

Selling Value Communications

Creative, dynamic and entrepreneurial development activities require communications focused on value. Data Strategy communications need to emphasise the benefits that the creativity, dynamism and entrepreneurial vision will bring. The communications needed should be tailored to the stakeholder audience's needs and should explain how the data initiative will fulfil these.

Sometimes a stick as well as a carrot is needed in these communications. For some initiatives, explaining the cost of inaction can be more compelling than describing the less tangible results. For example, a data activity that prevents the risk of a data breach or regulatory rule break is better described by outlining the consequences of non-compliance. In the case of General Data Protection Regulation (GDPR) breaches in Europe, authorities can levy fines up to 20 million euro or 4% of a company's global annual turnover whichever is greater. This compelling sum is enough to motivate even the most reluctant Board of Directors to take data privacy regulations seriously!

When devising Data Strategy communications, a mindset that is both technical and business oriented is needed. While it is important to outline some of the technical detail for the data activity being undertaken, too much detail on the technology or delivery process will confuse. Those inclined toward the technical need to remind themselves to emphasise the outputs and solution benefits. Similarly, the more business minded need to pay attention to not just focus on the benefits to be gained by their area, but to also recognise some of the process steps and delivery effort needed in securing any benefits. A Data Strategist is a new role in many organisations that lives and breathes this duality of mind.

A Data Strategist recognises that data itself is not insight or of significant value. It is a raw input yet to be developed and refined into value. The process to turn data into value needs to be successful and appropriate communications about that transformation can energise the delivery process itself. For example, data science projects can be exciting areas of innovation for many organisations today and talking about the benefits of data science use cases is a great way to engage stakeholders. Some caution is needed however, as data science projects are often over sold and the hypothesis pursued sometimes does not come true. Being clear about the risks while still communicating the potential benefits manages stakeholder expectations and more accurately reflects the nature of many data science projects undertaken.

Data Strategists help prioritise the way forward. They recognise that an organisation only has the capacity to deliver on a few fronts at any one time and so choices need to be made. And, these choices need to be sequenced for optimum effect. For example, new data sources may need to be secured, data architecture may need to be reinforced and data management practices may need to be improved, before the benefits of a new data platform can be fully exploited. The Data Strategist needs to balance the realities of the current situation with the ambitions for the future operating model, identifying the path that will deliver the right mix of foundational initiatives as well as much needed big value-adding initiatives to achieve the optimum results with the resources available.

Effective communications build confidence in the delivery journey of Data Strategy and we will discuss how to do this further in Chapter 2. Certainly, when describing the vision for Data Strategy, it needs to outline the long-term aspirations and benefits from the journey. Being honest and upfront about some of the difficulties and chances of success is needed, so that stakeholders can celebrate appropriately the many successes but are equally prepared for some of the difficulties and even occasional failures that may occur along the way.

Communications continue to be needed throughout the lifecycle of the Data Strategy. The initial communications to sell the anticipated value of the Data Strategy is important, but so too is the on-going communication during delivery and into more business-as-usual modes. Opportunities to remind stakeholders of the Roadmap and the value it brings to the organisation need to be systemised: so that the decision to proceed with new initiatives are actively promoted and the achievement of delivery milestones are celebrated.

Case Study: Securing buy-in to building Data Strategy value in a leading Insurer

The insurance sector is undergoing a data revolution at the current time. Many insurance companies have been drawn into the digital age through the need to work with aggregator online website businesses that bring together member insurance companies and showcase their offers for house, car, health, travel, etc. insurance products. Instead of the traditional offline business model, where customers walked into insurance brokers on high streets or conducted annual renewals via telephone or letter with their existing providers, customers now access a range of quotations from insurance companies following entering their details online. They are able to see for themselves the cheapest quotations and identify more clearly what drives the cost in their insurance premiums.

Due to aggregators, insurance businesses have had to build pricing engines to quickly offer the customers tailored quotations based on their circumstances, for example in the case of car insurance: age, home location, occupation, claims history, driving penalties, vehicle type and so forth. Additionally, to support these digital customers, they have needed to develop their call centres to answer renewal queries, take notifications of claims and manage related customer services (such as breakdown assistance, vehicle repair centres, replacement vehicle hire, window & tyre replacement services, etc.). As a result of new offers and services, they have needed to modify ways of working to be able to effectively manage staffing levels in call centre and back-office functions, measure customer satisfaction and continue to identify fraud across this ever-expanding digital footprint.

In a leading UK based vehicle insurance business, they faced a wide range of tantalising choices in addressing their next steps in their digital journey. So many options were open to them it was becoming increasingly difficult for them to know where best to start. To help decide the priority in the choices ahead a detailed assessment of each initiative was commissioned to define the appropriate implementation approaches, identify anticipated costs and resourcing required, review technology choices and the impact on existing data related activities, as well as to develop the business case for each initiative. Through this approach a clear path ahead was hoped to be seen.

For each initiative a project plan was produced and these were brought together into a combined Roadmap. The road mapping process was used to develop an appropriate prioritisation, balancing timelines with resource availabilities and costs with benefit delivery. It was also used as a method to secure the buy-in of stakeholders and communicate the approach to be followed across the organisation.

Projects that were foundational, such as improving Enterprise Architecture and building out a Master Data Management solution, were grouped into Foundational activities. Other projects that would be needed, for example, to support growth of new business in the next 12 months were planned to align with the related business strategy timetable. Longer-term initiatives to look at were timetabled for later in the Roadmap journey, such as aspects of Advanced Analytics and how they might support new business processes. Smaller scale Proof of Concept studies were also timetabled appropriately along the journey. Additionally, those initiatives with logical incremental linkages to each other were also highlighted. In this way a time-staged Roadmap over a three year period was produced – an example is shown in Figure 2 below.

The relative business value impact of each Data Strategy initiative is plotted against the relative readiness of the organisation to help ensure a realistic prioritisation is achieved. In the prioritisation, the relatively easy 'quick wins' and 'foundational initiatives' that were needed to be in place were identified so that they could be delivered early in the Roadmap and used as opportunities to demonstrate to stakeholders that progress was being delivered and thereby helping secure long-term buy-in to the Data Strategy.

This kind of illustrative Roadmap helped organisational stakeholders understand the sequence of activities contained within the Data Strategy, it also readily helped by categorising initiatives in terms of business impact and relative difficulty – thus giving some notion of effort / reward to readers of the Data Strategy.

Graphical single page images such as the Three Year Roadmap or a high-level logical Data Architecture drawing or a Data Model landscape or an image of a Data Team Organisational Chart are far more powerful and engaging to stakeholder than lengthy Word document descriptions. Similarly, Business Case timeline depictions, showing the projected cumulative costs and returns of Roadmap initiatives along the delivery calendar, and, where possible, clearly visible markers for when the Roadmap will 'break-even' and start making money, are all valuable tools in communicating with and securing buy-in from stakeholders.

DATA STRATEGY – SELLING THE VALUE

Figure 2: Example Three Year Roadmap

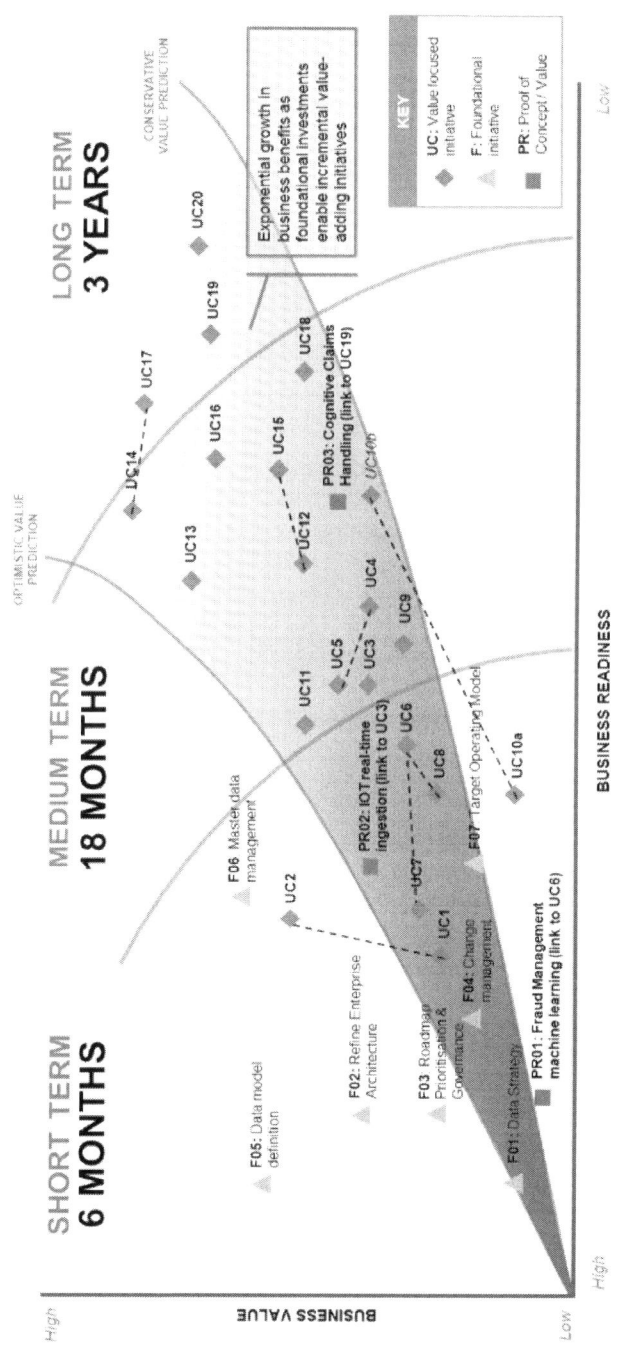

SELLING VALUE IS CREATIVE, DYNAMIC AND ENTREPRENEURIAL

CHAPTER 2: Know your audience

"Let's unlock the value of our data" is a call to arms in today's modern world for many organisations and a common refrain for many business leaders. Taking that call to arms and building out a Data Strategy that can be successfully implemented is the practical next step. However, developing a Data Strategy that resonates and has meaning for all in the organisation is not simple. A systematic approach to its writing is needed.

Selling "how Data Strategy is important" or, as I have referred to it, *Selling the Value* of Data Strategy, needs to be targeted differently for best effect with each stakeholder group. Some stakeholders prefer the black and white clarity of financial numbers: bringing them the comfort of simple return on investment analysis. Others have a stronger affinity for and are motivated by more intangible matters, such as capability improvements, up-skilling and better quality delivery: it is important to share with these the innovation path and knowledge gains to be achieved. In all cases, it is better to have a broad spread of benefits that meets the diverse spectrum of stakeholder needs.

C-suite Executives

The Chief Executives, Chief Marketing / Finance / Staff Officers, etc., as well as Chief Data / Information / Technology Officers, need to be able to demonstrate a Return on Investment from their Data Strategy. Any Data Strategy needs to justify the effort and expense in its roll-out and how its successful delivery will help support the organisation's strategy. Successfully delivering the organisation's Mission and or Purpose is the C-suite's primary concern, so the Data Strategy needs to be clearly aligned to that. The Roadmap needs to define the costs and benefits of the Data Strategy along the short-, medium- and long-term timeline. The value added needs to be clearly quantifiable and demonstrably achievable.

New innovations, new go-to-market propositions and new efficiencies need to be described in detail, outlining the rewards that can be achieved from their implementation as well as being clear on the investment needed to secure them. Even less-tangible rewards, such as better insights and even better decision making, need some description and quantification of why maintaining the status-quo is not satisfactory. The additional benefits achieved by improving speed and accuracy of decision making can be quantified. The downside of data breaches can be described and the magnitude of risks quantified.

For C-suite Executives, it is important to quantify as much as possible and provide estimates with upper and lower bound ranges if finding an exact number is not possible. This quantification can in turn be helpful when thinking about the priorities within the Data Strategy Roadmap, allowing stakeholders to clearly see quick wins and when added value will be delivered. By working with C-suite stakeholders, the right timing for the delivery of each data initiative can be set along the Roadmap to align with business needs.

Data Users

Data users want easier times. Easier times for data users usually come in the shape of new or improved tools, processes, data sets and outputs. Typically, data users are looking forward to the improvements promised in the Data Strategy. They want to perhaps move away from legacy tools to new more powerful technology that will make their work faster, more productive and allow for new improved outputs. They are often hopeful of the new and more efficient processes that will be adopted. They may also be excited by the opportunity to widen the scope of data being used in their jobs today and access new areas of information and insight.

For data users, quantifying the time saved from 'old world' to the 'new world' is an important sales message. Related to this it could also be important to talk about how much easier processes will be: for example, identifying how many spreadsheets can be decommissioned or data processing steps removed. Accuracy may be another alternative perspective to highlight, for example, what is the impact of removing error from decision making?

Data users also want marketable skills. A Data Strategy needs to address how to up-skill staff and needs to set out appropriate learning development paths for impacted employees. Getting the data users on board with the proposed changes comes from thinking through the practicalities of implementation from the data user perspective. From a change management perspective: providing skills-based training is clearly useful for the immediate task in hand, but providing training that is also recognised and makes the careers of the data users more marketable is going to be more readily welcomed. A Data Strategy that sets out to develop a positive data culture within the organisation and that enables continuous learning for staff, will be one that data users can more readily accept and want to be part of.

Data Processors

Data processors are similar to data users in many ways, as they too want easier times. Data processors are often faced with the impact of time-consuming data preparation activities, such as, poorly architected data structures, poor quality raw data, missing metadata and not-yet-validated master data. This data preparation effort takes time away from more value-adding data processing activities of Architects, Developers, Analysts, etc. A Data Strategy needs to address the anticipated efficiency gains and removal of waste from data processes. By drawing on Lean methodology, Data Strategy can provide stakeholders with great motivation to harness the benefits of process re-engineering.

Defining new ways of working are at the heart of Data Strategy. In particular, new ways of working will be required to embed new technology in the organisation. New data sets may need to be managed in new ways to ensure security, privacy and quality requirements. New organisational structures and data related teams may need to be set-up that require new management processes. New and or improved data architectures may need to be developed to better organise and structure data to be more efficiently and effectively managed. All such new ways of working should be defined to reduce risk: the risk of incorrectly deploying or using technology, the risk of inadequate protocols around the use of data resulting in data breaches that at one level produce inefficiencies and more seriously can lead to fines and commercial losses.

Governance of data processes is a key area of focus in any Data Strategy. Improved governance needs to be communicated to data processors and stakeholders in a positive manner: not additional controls for the sake of bureaucracy but for the delivery of improved more efficient and safer processes. The communication messages need to speak to the benefits that the strengthened governance system or new improved process will bring and how these will better secure the promised value add. If data processors and other stakeholders are to adopt these new processes it will help if they know why they are there and how the new ways of working support the effective delivery of the Data Strategy.

Data Owners and Data Stewards

Data Owners and Data Stewards have specific responsibilities in the governance of data processing and so, in addition to the above interests, often look at data related activities from a perspective of de-risking the handling of data and ensuring compliance.

The Data Owner is accountable for their data set, including: data definitions, data quality, data management policies, related processes and standards, security and privacy. They are the senior point of contact related to their data set, accountable to the Executive, and oversee others' use of their data set. As such they are particularly interested in data related approaches that make their role easier and that reinforce compliance in the use of their data set.

Likewise, Data Stewards live with the day-to-day operationalisation of data related activities related to their data sets and so will have vested interest in improvements to day-to-day ways of working and compliance. Perhaps above all other stakeholders, the Data Stewards will see acutely the cost of inefficiency and poor quality in data related activities. Therefore, securing their buy-in to changes will be key to the successful roll out of any new data related activities.

Resistance

Even the best described and well-articulated Data Strategy can meet with mistrust, inertia and resistance. The implementation of Data Strategy requires change and securing buy-in to change is never easy!

DATA STRATEGY – SELLING THE VALUE

For each Data Strategy activity, the new additional element of value needs to be fully described in words that mean something positive to the impacted stakeholders. Work on any additional proofs of that value may need to be undertaken to better secure stakeholder buy-in and de-risk delivery.

On-going communications during the roll-out of Data Strategy activities needs to be maintained to continue to reinforce the message that progress is happening as per the plan and value is being delivered incrementally as anticipated. A systematic Communications Plan, using a structure like that shown below in Figure 3, should be established to support this. Where delays to planned activities occur or even where an activity has failed to deliver, communications need also to be made to address the issue and what remedial actions will be taken. Similarly, where the Data Strategy needs to be adjusted or added to as new conditions are encountered or new requirements are identified, new communications will need to be produced for the stakeholders concerned.

If the benefits for change are clearly described and made compelling enough, stakeholder mistrust, inertia and resistance should be removed. A good understanding of the improvement levers that resonate with each stakeholder will help in this regard when defining the Data Strategy. Thereafter, the work done to conduct effective stakeholder analysis and develop a detailed stakeholder communication plan will continue to pay dividends during the implementation of the Data Strategy.

It is perhaps useful at this stage to remind the reader that over-selling a Data Strategy is just as problematic as under-selling one. Over committing, setting misleading expectations, developing un-feasible business cases, hiding delivery risks and so forth, do not help build trust and commitment with stakeholders. It is better to be realistic or potentially under-sell and over deliver, than risk alienating stakeholders with over-hyped and under-achieved promises. Failure to deliver leads to a loss in confidence and potentially having to write-off the costs of whole initiatives. All such failures can become significant barriers where significant re-work will be need to overcome mistrust for any subsequent Data Strategy deliveries.

Figure 3: Communications Plan Template

To whom?	Why?	How?	When?	By whom
• Who is the stakeholder audience?	• What are we communicating? • What are the communication objectives?	• What is the communication method?	• What is the timing / frequency of communication?	• Who is the communication author / source?

What is the value of Data Strategy?

An organisation's Data Strategy sets out to describe its data related assets that exist today and those that will be built going into the future. It describes how the organisation's data related activities will take place as well as describing the specific ways of working to be adopted in certain use cases. It sets out the data governance structures that will be used to manage data and its data processes. It also provides a clear Roadmap detailing the sequence of data related activities and the timelines for the delivery of the value defined in the Roadmap. Finally, it establishes how data will be monetised and what the business value-adding benefits will be.

Data encompasses all the information within an organisation and all the information flows coming in to and out of the organisation. It covers data that is in a stored state or in a transient state en-route to being stored or lost. This includes data that is historic, actual and predictive.

The value of data typically increases once it has been stored and transformed into insight. Until it has been transformed into value, it remains a raw material with limitless potential value but of limited actual value. This topic is further explored in Chapter 9.

Data assets are not limited to just the data itself. Those that work in the data transformation processes are human data assets and their work is expressed in terms of data capabilities (this is discussed further in Chapter 5). In addition to these human data assets, the technology deployed in the data transformation processes, the governance processes and architectural systems are all data related assets. All of these data related assets are described in the Data Strategy and how they come together in the delivery of data related activities is defined in the Data Strategy.

A Data Strategy without a Roadmap or plan for implementation is incomplete and remains just a 'dream'. As we will see in Chapter 9, a description of Industry 4.0 or IoT landscape or Advanced Analytics is just that: a narrative, however interesting. Only with a plan for how these and other aspects of the Data Strategy will be implemented and what benefits it will specifically bring to the organisation's stakeholders can the dream become reality.

Case Study: Targeted value communications in the Utility Sector

The Utility sector covers water, gas and electricity provision and profit-making enterprises in this sector face significant regulation in their delivery of services to the public. In England and Wales, the five year Asset Management Plan sets out the permissible price increases allowed by water companies and performance measures to be used by the regulator. Across the UK energy industry its regulator sets out RIIO (Revenue=Incentives+Innovation+Outputs) controls and funding over an eight year period, alongside price caps. These regulations stimulate a parallel internal business planning cycle: where investments, innovations and ways of working are organised. Data Strategy and its Roadmap are also planned within these boundaries and timelines. For example, processes to enable efficient and effective reporting on performance measures will be established ready for the start of the regulatory reporting period and used throughout. Any changes to this process would only be accepted on the basis that greater efficiency (i.e., cheaper delivery) is achieved.

Knowing this focus and fact that budgets are constrained within planned limits, reinforces the need for communications around Data Strategy and the Roadmap to clearly articulate the financial gains that any initiative will bring. This does not mean that capabilities cannot be improved or other intangible benefits improved, but it means that the primary communication messages must talk about cost savings generated and or income generated.

DATA STRATEGY – SELLING THE VALUE

In one water company a programme of Data Science work was initiated following careful consideration of the use case and benefits to be gained. Proofs of value were first conducted to demonstrate how the analytics would deliver cost savings. In one use case, additional sensors were deployed on to pumps at water treatment plants to monitor their correct functioning. This data was used to train the model to establish normal operation parameters for the pumps, real time data feeds could then be analysed to check if operational pumps were working within tolerances or if preventative maintenance repairs were needed. By monitoring pump sensor feeds and targeting maintenance work, breakdowns were significantly reduced and maintenance engineers were more efficiently deployed. The number of fines levied for environmental regulatory breaches caused by pumps not working properly was also significantly reduced. Over time, once the solution was rolled out across all the pump infrastructure in the network and across multiple years of operation, these benefits would then be multiplied.

This Data Science work was just part of the wider Data Strategy initiatives set out by the water company, but they were important use cases for demonstrating the value of Advanced Analytics in the business. Through the POV work and subsequent roll-out at scale, significant benefits could be identified. Communications about these benefits were targeted to the different stakeholder groups: first and foremost, for all groups was the reduction in regulatory-breach fines. More efficient engineer work patterns were also an important message for the maintenance teams. The collection and use of real-time engineering data were important for the IT team. The operationalisation of data science was a great use case for the Data Analytics team. The reduction of un-treated wastewater discharges due to broken pumps across the company network was an important message to customers as well as helping meet local environmental targets of the regulator.

To enable these communications, as well as the actual Data Science work itself, the related reporting for the different audiences with the different messaging was set-up. Developing these real-time dashboards and periodic performance snapshots, in this case using Microsoft Power BI, were just as important for stakeholders in some ways as they validated the investment in the delivery of the core Data Science solution.

CHAPTER 3: Understand your level of data maturity

Different areas of an organisation will have different levels of data maturity. By conducting a data maturity assessment, areas of relative strength and weakness can be identified. Data maturity assessments provide a visible path from early-stage deployments through to best-in-class adoption. How many steps or hierarchy levels there are along the maturity path depends on the exact data maturity assessment used. But by using a robust scoring mechanism at each level of maturity, allows the assessor to judge the organisation's performance and where it sits on the different aspects of the data maturity spectrum.

In practical terms, it is unlikely for an organisation to have a single level of maturity across all areas of assessment. Typically, on some aspects the organisation will be an early-stage adopter, but on others its deployments will be more advanced. Understanding this will help the assessor to identify what improvements are needed to move toward the next level of data maturity. In considering these potential improvement actions, the effort involved in their implementation can be weighed against the benefits gained and a value-based judgement can be assigned to each potential improvement. Not all of the potential improvements need to be implemented immediately. Usually, the foremost priorities are those that deliver the greatest value, but an appropriate plan needs to balance an organisation's data improvement maturity aspirations with the resources it has available to undertake them.

Thinking around potential data maturity improvements are valuable inputs to Data Strategy development. If a Data Strategy requirement can be delivered in conjunction with an aspect of data maturity improvement, this is clearly a win-win scenario.

What is data maturity?

Most Consultancy organisations have their own preferred data maturity model and assessment methodology. Some approaches are better than others, but all aim to deliver a rigorous and impartial view of how an organisation is using data to add value. Various different terminologies exist to describe levels of data maturity, here we will use the graphic below in Figure 4 as our guide.

Level 1: Adhoc – no common rationale, structure or process other than those used for individual specific projects. Analysis at this early stage tends to be restricted to descriptions of data, for example quantifying historic and actual data to describe what happened and is happening. Reporting delivers visualisations and enables data explorations to slice and dice findings. In terms of performance management, KPIs are tracked and alerts are set to warn of defined threshold breaches. Expertise is restricted to a few SMEs mostly in functional areas.

Level 2: Emergent – initial stage learnings are captured and a more systematic approach to data related activities is begun. Actual data is assessed and diagnostics are built based on past experience. Insights are developed to support current decision making. Exceptions and variety are analysed to build initial behaviour-based models. Some limited co-ordination and centralisation of data expertise is made to start building on learnings. Best practice examples deliver quantifiable benefit from data related work across a single business process.

Level 3: Predictive – the question of what could and will happen is addressed in a systematic manner. Analytics builds forecasts, what if analysis for different scenarios and behaviour-based propensity models. Reporting adds trend analysis, highlights performance gaps from plans and variations in different cohorts within data sets. Dedicated Reporting and Analytics teams are managed to become engine rooms of insight. Data systems start to receive significant investment in their own right and architectures start to be proactively managed to enable more successful delivery. Best practice examples deliver a data driven business wide transformation.

Level 4: Prescriptive – learnings are used to chart next best actions and target better outcomes. Data is used to start to optimise business-as-usual processes. Continuous improvement is leveraged via Machine Learning models. New sources of data start to be systematically captured including customer, supplier and employee behaviour data and these are integrated into the insights of the

DATA STRATEGY – SELLING THE VALUE

Figure 4: From information to optimisation through improved data analytics maturity

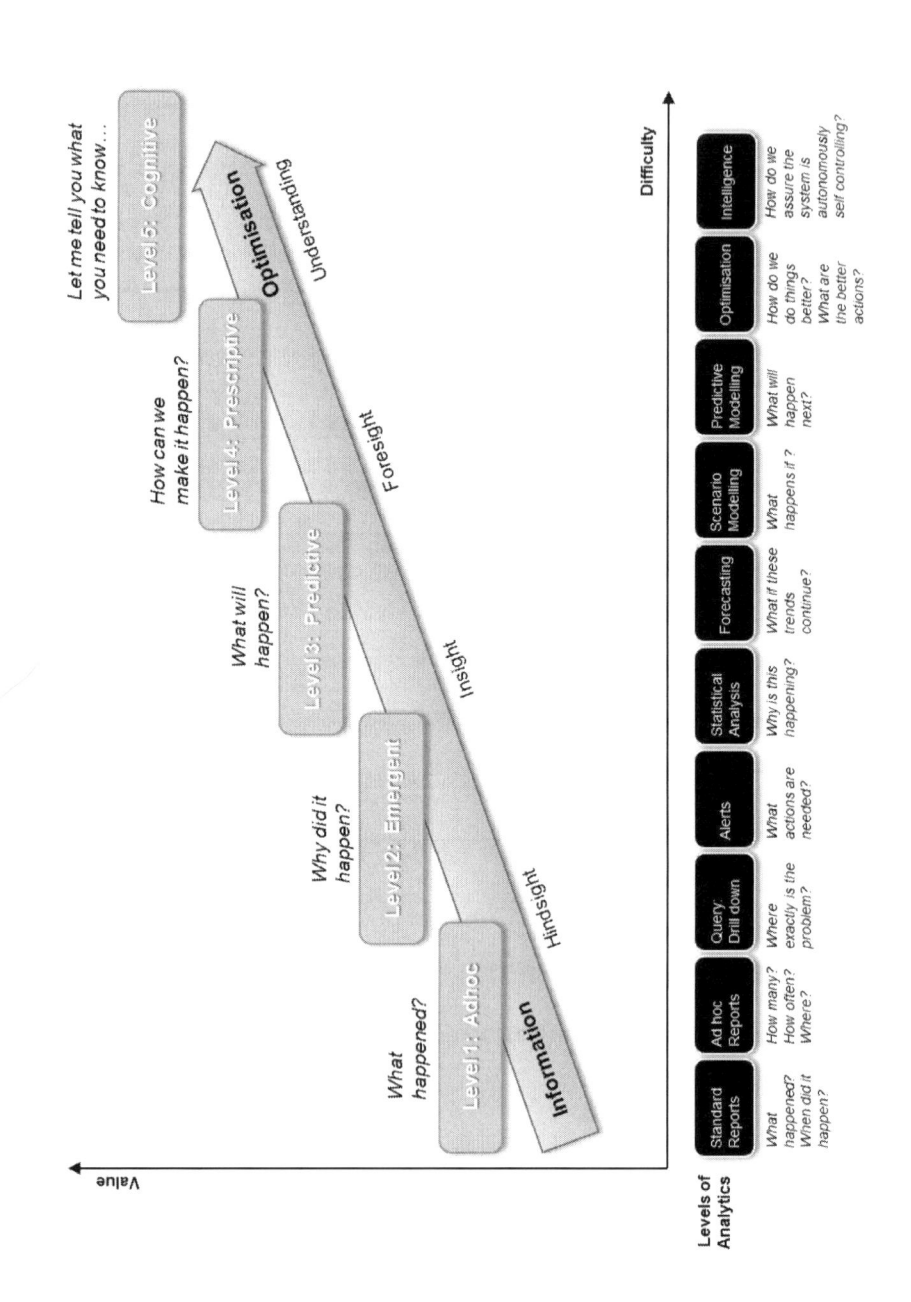

UNDERSTAND YOUR LEVEL OF DATA MATURITY

organisation. Data Analytics encompasses more real-time streaming data, IoT and incorporates visual, sound and environmental inputs in its models. Data quality improvement initiatives are established. Board level appointments for Data are established with dedicated Heads of data governance, architecture, security, strategy, etc. Best practice examples deliver data enabled organisation metamorphosis.

Level 5: Cognitive – autonomous routines are established and data assets are secured. Data is automatically feeding Artificial Intelligence solutions that are an integral part of business-as-usual operations. Data related activities are seen as a source of Intellectual Property that needs protection and periodic control to ensure on-going optimisation. A data culture pervades the organisation and staff are encouraged to continue to learn data related skills. On-going improvements to data quality are proactively pursued. Business acquisitions are made to enhance existing data models and evidence-based go-to-market propositions. Best practice examples build on the early-stage Digital business and enhance its ethical data driven business model.

The practicalities of data maturity assessment delivery

Different perspectives on organisational performance need to be gathered from an appropriate range of different stakeholders when conducting a data maturity assessment. It is important to not just look from one perspective but have a rounded view of performance. C-suite Executives have a key input in describing whether an organisation's data related activities are delivering what is needed today and where gaps exist. Users and Consumers likewise can describe well what benefits they have from using or consuming data related products and where weaknesses exist. Developers and Product Owners can talk to the strengths and weaknesses of the delivery processes and data related capabilities that exist within the organisation. Data Stewards can help identify some of the data governance achievements and challenges to be addressed.

During stakeholder data maturity assessment interviews, the participants perspectives can be gathered on actual performances as well as perspectives on aspirational performance. Actual performances are captured in response to a set of specific calibrated questions that distinguish performance on a scale of low to high complexity and value add. These views can then be benchmarked against performances of those of other organisations, including peers within the same industry, whose performance has been measured using the same calibrated questions and scale. In this way, the maturity assessment provides internal stakeholders with a calibrated assessment of their own perspectives against the external benchmark of peer organisations.

Responses to the Data Maturity assessment questions are collected from each participant. Individual questions are grouped under categories of enquiry and an average score across all questions in a category is calculated. These scores are averaged across responses from all participants for each category. In turn an average score across all categories is calculated to arrive at a final single Data Maturity Assessment score. This final score is used to then position the organisation on the appropriate point in the data maturity hierarchy.

To capture participants views on where improvement priorities should be focused, the same Data Maturity Assessment questions can be used to identify not only existing performances but also aspirationally where the organisation should be. When looking at the aspirational scores, it is interesting to analyse the degree of commonality and diversity in the participants scoring. Sometimes stakeholders' views on their aspirations for data related activities can be surprisingly aligned. Where this is the case, it provides a particularly strong basis for agreeing change and a valuable input to the Data Strategy Roadmap.

Building a Roadmap to improvement

The data maturity assessment identifies an organisation's current state of data related performance and the steps needed to improve. To bring these steps to life however and make these steps more tangible for organisational stakeholders, a tailored Roadmap is needed.

The Data Strategy Roadmap sets out the short-, medium- and longer-term plan of data related activities. It covers more than just a wish-list of new and exciting technologies that could be procured. It focuses on the complete set of capabilities needed to secure business benefits and it prioritises these over time.

A Data Strategy Roadmap is not written once and then set in stone never to be amended again. Instead, it is a living programme of work with clear timelines, milestones and outcomes all of which are reviewed periodically to check if the delivery is on track, whether mitigating action is needed or a Roadmap adjustment is needed. Returning to the Data Maturity Assessment and repeating it annually can be a useful tool in demonstrating improvement to key stakeholders, particularly those who need confidence that the Roadmap is delivering the benefits sought.

The contents of the Data Strategy Roadmap need to sell the benefits of its implementation to stakeholders. Stakeholders' expectations also need to be managed as not everything can necessarily be achieved at the same time. The timelines and prioritisation of the data related activities will need to be agreed with stakeholders with care. A realistic plan is needed. Implementation delays will not build trust and overly long programmes of work will not keep the positive momentum for change. Agile delivery can be an effective mechanism to demonstrate progress and build trust.

Improving maturity immediately across all areas is unlikely to be realistic, particularly so given ever present budget constraints. Instead, a more logical and targeted sequence of incremental improvement will be easier to manage and more likely to succeed. Prioritisation should be given to the greatest value-adding deployments. Initial areas of focus should also be made on enabling capabilities that will provide a foundation on which future development can be built.

It is important to also realise that an organisation is unlikely to be or need to be best in class on all aspects: different areas of the business for example may never need to go beyond level 3 and perhaps only a handful of use cases may make commercial sense to ever get to level 5. Investment needs to be determined by the value gained and not everything will make business sense to be improved at the same pace or to the same level.

An example Three Year Roadmap was shown in Chapter 2: Figure 1 and an alternative view is shown below in Figure 5. In this Roadmap type, the Data Strategy initiatives are grouped under four vectors that lead toward a Data Strategy Vision, namely: Data Platform, Data & Analytics Solutions, Capability & People, Communications & Education. The delivery of the

DATA STRATEGY – SELLING THE VALUE

Figure 5: Example Data Strategy Roadmap by Delivery Theme

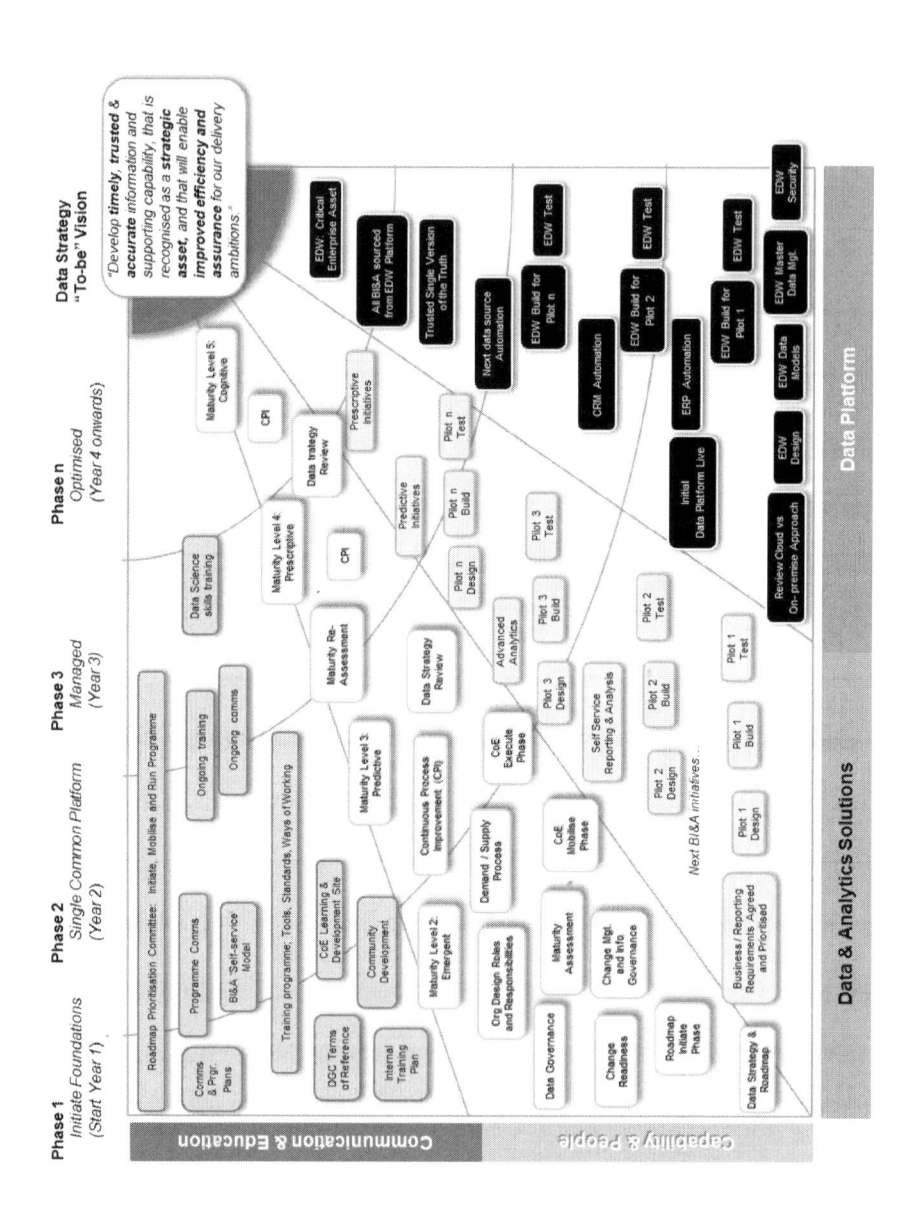

initiatives within each of these vectors, when combined, progress the organisation in its journey toward the Vision. And, the sequencing by phase indicates, broadly, the passage of time, but no definitive guide is provided as to when initiatives will definitively be delivered or when the Data Strategy Mission will be completed.

Roadmap progress measurement

Just as a Roadmap needs to identify the key deliverables across its timeline, for each deliverable a more detailed project or programme plan is needed. These individual project or programme plans need to include clearly defined goals, performance KPIs and reporting. These measurement mechanisms need to be sufficient to adequately communicate the on-going success or not of the project or programme. The degree of the sophistication in the project or programme performance will depend on its scale and level of risk faced by non-delivery. High profile mission critical projects or programmes will need more elaborate and frequent reporting than those that are lower impact data related initiatives.

A Roadmap Prioritisation Committee is best established to review the ongoing delivery of the Roadmap and typically sets-up a Project Management Office function to oversee this task. Reports on the progress of each individual Project on the Roadmap can then be monitored. Communications around the successful delivery of anticipated benefits can be made and any mitigating actions can be taken as needed.

Agile delivery mechanisms provide regular drops of value normally at the end of each Sprint. Projects are broken into a subset of stories that when combined deliver the total value and benefit sought by the Product Owner of the data related initiative. Each Sprint delivers a story that the Product Owner tests and needs to sign off acceptance. The delivery of a Sprint also contains a number of ceremonies that the Product Owner participates in and so Agile is set-up to provide visibility of development progress through its lifecycle. Agile delivery is also set-up to incorporate learning and improvement, for example, normally at the end of each Sprint, a retrospective ceremony is held to review lessons learned that will be beneficial when acted on in future Sprints.

Case Study: Building Data Maturity in the Airline industry

A leading European airline operator has set itself an ambition to become a Digital Airline. In many ways it was not a stranger to digital ways of working. It had among other developed an industry leading online booking platform that incorporated sophisticated pricing algorithms. But, moving beyond its existing online booking system, it wanted to expand its digital footprint across all ways of working and all areas of the business. When I spoke with them about this ambition, it was clear that they realised such a change could not happen overnight, but they did want to proactively manage progress so that it could happen soon. They wanted the transformation to be systematically planned and scheduled over time so that there was clear visibility of achieving each step in the journey.

The airline also recognised that they needed a clear baseline understanding of their current performances on which to plan improvements. They asked me to provide them with an independent assessment. Together we selected an appropriate Analytics Maturity Assessment Framework to be used as the methodology for capturing this baseline. There are a number of Maturity Assessment tools in existence, but the version selected was particularly powerful as it supported peer benchmarking. Not only would their data related activities be scored on a structured basis, but their overall maturity scores could be compared to a number of other peer businesses.

The maturity assessment was conducted over a period of 3 weeks through structured interviews with 30 different members of staff from across the organisation: End-users, Executives, Data Owners, Data Stewards, Analysts, Developers and Architects. In this way quantitative as well as qualitative evidence could be established and a real image, good and bad, of the airline's current levels of performance captured. Quantitative scoring was powerful as it provided an impartial mechanism to judge performances. Scores removed ambiguity, they helped participants distinguish between performance levels and allowed for aggregate scores to be produced (helping nuance some outlier opinion). Qualitative commentary, presented in a confidential manner, was a particularly powerful way to get to the heart of certain issues, define behaviours and highlight aspirations. Based on the evidence gathered, a data maturity score was established and a series of recommendations for improvement actions were identified. These findings were presented to business leaders and a report was disseminated to participants and other stakeholders. Many of these actions were incorporated into the annual business planning cycle of relevant departments and performance metrics were defined and used to track implementation.

The following year, the same maturity assessment was re-run with a different set of respondents from across the airline and with a view to understanding if the actions had been implemented and if maturity had moved forward. Re-running the maturity assessment on a year-on-year basis was very valuable. It established this impartial structured monitoring tool as part of the business-as-usual governance processes, it demonstrated confidence and commitment by leaders in the digital journey the airline was on, and it helped focus attention on targeting successful incremental maturity improvements. From a Data Strategy perspective, the data maturity assessment effectively became a performance benchmark. On the one hand, it checked that progress was happening in the shape of successfully delivering Data Strategy initiatives, on the other, it verified that these initiatives were not only providing business value, but also that the organisation was improving its data capabilities.

CHAPTER 4: Implement Technology but not just for Technology's sake

To date, a lot of transformation has been driven by technology. Today however, we find ourselves at the point where transformation is being driven by data and the business value add that data can bring. Don't get me wrong: new and improved technology will continue to appear in the marketplace bringing new additional benefits to the user. Periodic reviews and road tests of this technology we use is helpful, but care needs to be taken to not over emphasize technology as being the sole solution to a data related problem.

Too many organisations expend too much time and energy implementing new technology and not enough time and energy getting the most from the technology they already have. It is important to get the balance right between maintaining out of date legacy tech and embarking on what is often a relatively expensive tech refresh.

Lowering the initial cost of technology has been a key market development in recent years as demonstrated by the commercial models of Cloud and Software-as-a-Service (SaaS) technology. The use of Cloud and its consumption-based pricing model is revolutionising the ease of setting-up and scaling data platforms. Likewise, the move to SaaS technology can help reduce the immediate cost of ownership. In either case however, the benefits from the use of these technologies and their benefits need to be assessed. Any new technology deployment can often entail significant cost and time that takes focus away from doing the real work of fully using the existing technology available. In this case, it really is not the technology that is important, but what outputs you secure from it.

Use technology to drive value

The best investment case for new technology is when the new technology allows for new business propositions to be delivered that were not previously possible. To an extent all technology should work assuming the basic assumptions were right, otherwise why was it being considered for purchase in the first place? Arguments should be less about this technology or that technology, but more about this additional value add that the former brings versus the later. Certainly, arguments that demonstrate that the new technology will provide new capabilities to deliver some new business value are the most compelling. Here it should be easy to build a business case that establishes the value of the new proposition, for example the quantification of the increase in sales.

People use technology, so it is important to consider the investment needed in up-skilling existing staff or recruiting new staff to use the new technology in addition to the technology costs alone. Re-training and recruitment take time and cost, so both aspects need to be factored into the new technology deployment timelines. Some skills are more expensive to come by than others, for example data science skills typically take many years to develop, so are at a market premium. Technology that is at the cutting edge of innovation will require investment in staff capable of its adoption. Bearing this in mind, depending on where an organisation is located or how much it wishes to pay staff, may mean the size of the talent pool within which it can search for staff to join its organisation is more limited.

The one thing that is certain is that technology choices will continue to change. In today's fast-moving world, technology is starting to get out of date within three years and becomes a legacy technology within five years. This pace of change means organisations should be planning to adapt: testing and rolling-out new tech, optimising maximum value from existing tech, as well as managing the retirement and cut-over of legacy tech. A technology plan that covers its full lifecycle is needed.

The pandemic has changed how the world works. The shift to remote working has encouraged a move away from some technologies and the adoption of others. The reliance on physical hardware is being replaced by a more Cloud centric approach. Organisations have been aware of legacy systems, but now the priority to address these has shot-up the agenda. Data and System migration has firmly moved toward the top of many organisation's Data Strategy Roadmap.

New thinking around technology should be taken into consideration. The SaaS model has transformed the debate around cost of ownership from a traditional model, which had a high upfront cost and a smaller on-going cost thereafter, to a new pay-as-you-go model, which has smaller regular payment schedules over time that can be scaled up or down depending on use. Likewise, best practice technology architectures also change. Modern technology architecture thinking has changed to embrace, for example, distributed computing in data platform architecture and federated learning in Artificial Intelligence models. New ways of working will continue to point toward the limits in traditional thinking and organisations will need to continuously check how these changes impact their approach to technology. Best practice architectural practices, such as DCAM, Dmbok or TOGAF, defined and discussed further in Chapter 6, provide valuable input to the way data should be handled optimally. Although differences in approach exist in these architectural frameworks, they should nevertheless help ensure that any technology deployed is used more efficiently and effectively.

Alignment of the Technology Inventory to tooling that allows the organisation to move forward along the data maturity curve will deliver a win-win. Technology that delivers fast-track access to prescriptive and cognitive solutions should be prioritised for trial. Technology that supports greater degrees of automation, perhaps through the use of IoT, Machine Learning and Artificial Intelligence, should be tested to see if their deployment will deliver significant returns.

Technology costs more than the initial purchase price

It is easy to think about technology costs in terms of the initial purchase price, but the real cost of technology is generally greater than just that. Commonly, technology today comes with additional support and maintenance costs. These are typically a percentage of the initial purchase price payable annually on the anniversary of that purchase. An example of these are software licence models among BI or ERP vendors. Alternative technology supply models have a consumption based commercial model where different fees are charged depending on the amount or level of utilisation. Examples of these are Cloud platforms such as Amazon Web Services, Google, Microsoft Azure or, relatively new entrant, Alibaba.

Additional to the actual technology licence, subscription and consumption costs, there is the cost of deployment to consider. Often, the technology cost itself is cheap in comparison to the on-going cost of the technology deployment. Deployment costs cover the staff needed to install, run and support the technology over its lifetime. This cost also includes the investment needed in setting-up new processes that the new technology requires to be effective. The value from the technology however comes from the deployment, so the more widely the technology is deployed typically the more value is gained, but of course at the same time the greater the deployment costs are.

Costs of deployment include the cost of conducting any initial proof of value or concept, then the subsequent first deployment, then the set-up of the business-as-usual team(s) to use and run the technology, the set-up and running of any user support service, the creation of back-up and contingency solutions, training costs and certifications fees, technology updates and version releases, as well as the eventual decommissioning programme.

Given these extensive costs that are likely to be incurred with each technology implemented, it is important to not get caught up in the excitement of procuring technology like a latest fashion item. Having a Technology Inventory that includes the anticipated lifecycle helps planning for an appropriate technology budget. Knowing when to seek external advice on technology choices can speed up the selection process for new technology and help avoid some of the pitfalls that exist. It is important to get the balance right from moving too soon and leaving legacy technology too long in place. Instead, building-up some standard approaches and periodic reviews will be beneficial.

Focus on core principals

Establishing some standard rules around technology deployments will pay dividends in effective technology management. Following nine core principals, as described below, should enable effective technology management.

1) Produce and maintain a Technology Inventory that lists out the existing technologies within the organisation, when they were introduced and the anticipated timings for review and replacement.
2) Agree a realistic budget in line with the Technology Inventory and track expenditure.

3) Review the use of technologies of the same type with a view to rationalising to a core set. Manage these as a Tools Portfolio.
4) Proactively decommission technology. Don't leave technology to become legacy and, where technology is in active use, periodically check whether all the licences / services are needed or if services can be turned-off.
5) Invest in fully exploiting the technology you have; deploy it widely; work with vendors to investigate how the benefits gained in one area can be scaled and captured again elsewhere in the organisation.
6) Review options around use of third-party partners. What is core capability that must be kept in house and what may be commercially more viable to outsource? Can use of third-party partners bring access to cheaper resources (perhaps via the use of less expensive off-shore resources) or a pool of more expert staff (which would de-risk aspects of technology delivery)?
7) Proactively review back-up plans for when technology fails or is compromised. Deployments can fail, who guarantees they don't? What security exists around mission critical technology and their outputs? How is core data protected? Are your data centres backed-up? What are the service levels for critical technology?
8) Proactively track benefits gained from technology. Have benefits gained been greater than anticipated?
9) Test innovative technology on an on-going basis. How well can new technology deliver previously uncaptured business value? How can new technology help us move forward in data maturity? How can technology help us bring economies by automating some of our processes?

Remember that new technology is accompanied by new ways of working

To be effective, the deployment of new technology needs to also embrace new ways of working. New processes are likely to be needed and sometimes it will be beneficial to create whole new organisational structures.

Project teams will need to be set-up and invested in to establish new processes and carry-out staff training. Centres of Excellence may need to be built to manage organisation-wide deployments. New functional teams and units may need to be formed, for example, data scientists and other subject matter experts might be brought together in an Advanced Analytics team.

Roles and responsibilities will also change as new technology is introduced. In the case of SaaS, administration rights will need to be defined and traditional procurement authorities will need to be devolved away from Financial Controllers and commercial buying teams to Technologists. Processes will need to be modified, as no longer will purchase decisions need to be signed off by Procurement, but now Admins will have the flexibility to increase or decrease services and instantly change expenditures. In many organisations this represents a huge shift: devolving budgetary control and responsibilities to new parties.

Technology choices will also change the culture of the organisation. Selecting to use one technology will bring with it a group of people that are invested in that technology. For example, a Microsoft team is different in make-up and style to an Amazon Web Services team and an Oracle team is different to a SAP team. Staff invest throughout their careers in understanding and building up expertise in using certain technologies. While some skills are transferable, others are not and so barriers to entry build up over time for certain staff based on the technology choices made.

Adding similar technologies in parallel to the first for specific use cases is a path followed by some larger organisations, but of course this dilutes the return on investment from the initial technology selected and adds to the administrative burden of now managing two technologies effectively. Competing technologies being used by different teams in the same organisation reduces the opportunity for synergy, shared learnings and economies of scale. Thankfully, most organisations generally see the benefit of rationalising technologies around a common core set. And to encourage this, to support customer loyalty and the growing variety of data use cases, most Data Platform vendors invest considerably in developing a rich range of powerful tooling for their community.

In addition to the impact that technology has on ways of working, the way data architecture is implemented will have equally significant impact. Data Modelling is discussed in Chapter 10, but it should be clear that how a data model is implemented as a living data architecture will also impact the ways of working. For example, is a single Data Lake or Enterprise Data Warehouse to be built or will multiple specific data stores be maintained? Will there be one common Master Data Repository or will there be multiple systems containing sources of Master Data?

How to quantify the value of Technology related activities

The good thing about deciding to replace old technology with new is that an assumption has been made that the old technology is not good enough or that the new technology is so much better. This assumption provides an opportunity to conduct a proper assessment of the value you currently gain from using existing technology and that foreseen from new technology. It provides the opportunity to speak with users of the technology, to examine the ways of working with that technology, and in doing so it should be possible to understand the benefits gained from its use as well as the costs. Likewise, the costs for the new technology should be readily available, who will be using it should be known and a view should be possible to formulate on the anticipated benefits to be gained.

When it comes to technology costs, it is important to remember to include full-life-time costs. These costs include the initial purchase/subscription price, implementation cost, running costs, support costs and anticipated end of life costs. It is also important to include the associated costs with the technology deployment: for example, the cost of end user training.

So far, so simple. Where technology cost-benefit analysis gets more complicated is around quantifying the value add of some of the more intangible benefits. Let's take an example of a new BI tool: how do you quantify the benefit of better decision making? Here it is important to do more work on defining what better means: for example, does better mean faster? In which case, take the anticipated use cases for the BI tool and work through how much faster the new tool will enable the reporting of insight to end users. Once this is defined, make an appropriate assessment of the benefit of this shorter timeframe on the organisation for that use case. It could be at this stage, that the benefit gained from going faster is found to be quite small: in which case, an alternative benefit hypothesis is needed or the chances are that the use case identified is not really much of a value add use case and some further reflection on potentially more impactful use cases is needed. Other similar words to 'better', like de-risk, improve, etc. need further breakdown and analysis to allow appropriate benefit hypotheses to be defined and tested against. Analysts use the "3 Why's" to drill down to root causes and help focus on the true meaning in statements. Returning to our example: i. *Why* is better decision making beneficial? ii. *Why* is faster time to insight beneficial? iii. *Why* does almost real-time reporting with zero FTE involved in delivery beat the existing reporting process?

Security needs to be considered throughout Technology related activities

The impact of new technology should be considered from a security perspective. There are obvious access rights questions that need to be addressed, such as, who has access, who administers, who maintains, etc. These are relatively straight forward to manage; and increasingly, active directory is being used as the single accreditation hub to manage individual's permissions while supporting single sign-on. Systematically managing individual and group permissions is fundamental to effective security management.

Technology today is itself also getting better at tracking who is accessing, when and what they are doing with the technology. This tracking often comes with roll-back functionality to return to previous states and versions. The installation of up-to-date virus/malware protection software similarly helps check and safeguard data and tooling from hackers and malicious third parties.

Another aspect of security related to technology is the need to ensure system availability. System availability at one level relates to 'break-fix' services, where for some technologies they will need to be near 100% available at all times and for other less critical technologies lower levels of availability will be acceptable. Likewise, critical data sets will require backed-up copies to be stored and for other data sets it may be acceptable that they are not saved, overwritten or destroyed almost immediately. It is important therefore to know where data is located, what it contains and who has access to it.

To measure the effectiveness of security in your organisation, it is important to conduct a regular Data Security Risk assessment: typically carried out on an annual basis. Security Risk Assessments are vital to establishing current security gaps and making recommendations for breach prevention. They also will check that the security requirements found in many regulations are considered as part of a comprehensive approach to security. The Security Risk Assessment will identify what are the current risks the organisation is exposed to. These include items such as access, user behaviour, data criticality, data and technology availability, etc. In assessing risk, the assessment will categorise data, systems and data related activities by the degree of risk associated with it. By so doing, any recommendations from the risk assessment can be prioritised for remedial action.

Case Study: A data platform fiasco in the Fast-Moving Consumer Goods sector

A famous global clothing brand was reviewing its data architecture with a view to introducing a new data platform technology. This particular brand had been established some 100 years ago and over its many years of operation had built-up a range of different architectural types, often built-in silos for specific isolated purposes, and using a range of different technologies. Like many organisations operating today, their architectural estate could be described as a sprawl: with some good parts, but unfortunately a lot of legacy.

Fast moving consumer goods companies however, as the name implies, need to respond fast. In today's rapidly changing world, consumer fashions are moving faster than ever before. The speed of change is driven by global media, the growing importance of internet influencers in shaping trends and competitors improving their supply chains and operations to respond to and make the most of market opportunities. All of these factors mean improving the digitalisation of FMCG businesses to better identify and respond to changing demand can only be a positive.

Returning to the famous brand, the idea to improve architectures to better support business operations was therefore a positive development. Unfortunately, the way it addressed its requirements did not deliver success. A small team was tasked to find out the costs of each leading data platform technology: AWS, Google and Microsoft Azure. They went through a desk-top exercise to distil some meaningful cost estimates for an imaginary use case. Okay so far as it goes, but unfortunately their enquiries stirred interest from platform vendors: provoking numerous communications, support partners being engaged and interested parties being approached. The competition to secure their business was on!

The team had unwittingly managed to create a huge amount of market interest based on an unknown or at best an unclear set of requirements. Even the vendors' and support partners' offers to help were in fact not helping, as the business had not yet stood back and established what success might look like. What was the business case they had for this initiative? Did they want just another data platform to achieve this use case (effectively adding a new platform to those already in their architecture estate) or did they want to remove one or more of their existing platforms? What skills did the organisation have in using the different platform technologies? Were they planning on implementing the platform themselves or would they outsource this activity to a support partner? The list of possible questions goes on!

In this case, the rush to get an answer to the cost of technology was far too early. Without first defining the requirement and foremost understanding the anticipated business value to be achieved, the answers to questions on technology costs and abilities were meaningless. Rather than being able to efficiently engage with suppliers their approach generated confusion and waste for all involved. Our global clothing brand was not able to move forward at the time with a new data platform and securing the much-needed business benefits from the new technology were delayed.

Contrast this sad tale to that of other retailers, particularly those of online only retailers, such as eBay, Ocado or Wayfair. These have established and continue to invest in the development of an integrated platform that supports their digital business model end-to-end. They systematically review the entirety of their data architecture, proactively identify areas for further development in a planned manner and incrementally develop value-added features.

CHAPTER 5: Think People

Data Strategy is implemented by people for people. The Data Strategy needs to focus on what the business value will be for stakeholders and how people will work to achieve that. In this Chapter we will see that there is no single Target Operating Model for successful Data Strategy delivery, but there are key roles to consider and typical structures that support people in their implementation of Data Strategy.

Taking your people on the Data Strategy journey is pivotal to success. All too often a Data Strategy fails because stakeholders lose confidence in its journey and the value promised. Sometimes this is because it takes too long to be deployed, sometimes it is because what is being deployed is not really what is wanted. Reinforcing to stakeholders what they have achieved so far and reminding them of what is still to come should help assuage fears. Providing regular communications on the progress and delivery of the promised value of data related activities should help secure stakeholders on-going commitment.

Building an ethical data culture within the organisation will provide the foundation on which future success is built. Staff that buy-in to the ethical data culture and see the merit of its application in the ways of working within the organisation will be proactive supporters or agents of change.

Be realistic about people capabilities

When thinking about the people aspect of Data Strategy it is important to start with an assessment of the current state of peoples' data related capabilities. Based on this it will be possible to judge the gap between existing capabilities and the capabilities needed to achieve the different aspects of the Data Strategy.

Once the size and nature of the capability gap is assessed, how best to bridge the gap can be worked on. There are four main resourcing options available and the fourth is perhaps the most common.

1) **Grow your own people** – given a Data Strategy is effectively a long-term commitment to embrace data you would think that most organisations would automatically seize the opportunity to invest in their human resources. Unfortunately, this is not always the case. Some organisations fear that their staff are not good enough or, most commonly, will not adapt quickly enough. This may be true in part, but nevertheless if the Data Strategy is to turn data into a commercial differentiator over time, organisations will need to accept that their staff must be up-skilled and learn to take a lead in the data journey. Certainly, the pursuit of a Data Strategy that invests in the skills and continuous learning of staff, is one which staff should more readily engage with and want to be a part of.

   Mobilising staff around technology deployments and up-skilling them in that technology is an obvious first step. Building on staffs' existing competences and investing in on-the-job training or online training programmes can be a relatively inexpensive way to improve capabilities. Train the trainer programmes are particularly cost-effective methods to scale the roll-out of new capability learnings.

2) **Recruit third parties** – the buying-in of ready qualified expertise is the fastest way to mobilise. This could be anything from the permanent employment of a handful of experienced recruits to the establishment of whole new teams to fast-track development in a specific area.

   Contract staff are also a highly used option, where expertise is brought in for a finite period of time and then let go at the end. Contractors are often used as a half-way house between full outsourcing of an activity and full own team delivery, where some key roles within a delivery team are filled by temporary staff working alongside permanent staff. The use of contract staff can be a good option, however the expertise gained is only temporary and as soon as the Contractor departs, that knowledge can be lost. Contractor roles are also usually more expensive than full time employees.

3) **Outsource** – for areas which are deemed non-core to the business, outsourcing of some data related activities is a particularly

valuable approach. For example, the delivery of a 24/7 help desk for users of a Business Intelligence technology may be deemed non-core and in fact a third-party partner might be more cost effective in the running of such a service. The key to these outsourcing decisions is the definition of core and non-core. Understanding points of market differentiation is important in making this judgement and technology that supports key market propositions is generally better managed by in-house staff and processes.

4) **Hybrid** – given the wide nature of technology and data related activities a hybrid approach to staffing is frequently the chosen path. Here staff, work alongside a mix of third-party options in the delivery of the Data Strategy. Following this hybrid route is fine, but a regular review of the mix of resourcing is needed if the organisation is to in-source data literacy and grow an ethical data culture over time. Over reliance on external third parties, however good, will detract from strengthening internal capabilities and may slow the success of Data Strategy delivery as a whole.

Data roles and responsibilities

Regardless to the approach taken to resourcing, the roles and responsibilities of staff working on data related activities are the same. There are different roles needed to deliver your Data Strategy successfully, these include: data owners, data stewards, data processors and data users.

Data Owners are responsible for a specific dataset (or sets) within your organisation and their responsibilities include the quality assurance aspects related to this data set as well as the ultimate authority for questions around modifications, definitions, usage, etc. of their data set.

Data Stewards are responsible for the day-to-day utilisation and management of data sets in general. Their responsibilities include day-to-day management assurance and guidance on the best practices of usage regarding data. They will be interested in assuring the use of common standards, methods, processes, etc., to build good practices.

Data Processors are responsible for their discrete part within the ongoing ingestion, storage, transformation and output development activities within the organisation. Typically, data processors work in teams with each team member having specific areas of responsibility within the data related activity value chain.

Data Users are the group of people that actively consume data. Data users' consumption of data includes all data needed for reporting, analytics and applications within the organisation. They can be perceived as the customer of the data related activity.

It is perhaps useful to note here that the above role definitions differ from those used in the Information Security and Data Protection domain, where Data Stewards and Data Processors in particular have specific responsibilities not necessarily included above.

When implementing a data related activity, it is important that the above roles are clearly attributed to individuals. In some data related activities, for example around General Data Protection Regulations (GDPR) in Europe, these roles have legal implications. Knowledge of the roles and responsibilities as defined by regulations is paramount. Increasingly businesses have started to introduce an overarching Board level appointment of a Chief Data Officer (CDO) to bring together responsibility for all data related activities within the organisation. Once appointed, the CDO often nominates a specific individual 'Data Strategist' within the organisation or from an independent Consultancy to work with all relevant stakeholders and author the Data Strategy.

Be ambitious with your people, but avoid pitfalls

In order to future proof your organisation ready for tomorrow's challenges, an investment in the development of staff capabilities is needed. Staff need to be allowed sufficient time within their duties to train and learn new skills. Learning also comes with a degree of management needing to accept some failure. New skills are not acquired in one go, but often need to be acquired and improved over time. Allowing people to test their learnings, including sometimes failing in their implementation, as long as within safe boundaries, supports the learning process. Similarly, just as new technology choices sometimes don't achieve their anticipated successes, likewise some staff may not rise to the challenge that a particular learning requires. Understanding and management across this learning process will be needed.

Continuous professional development and certification around technologies can be a valuable part in motivating and showing investment in staff. Likewise improving data literacy among end users of data solutions will pay dividends. Enabling end-users to become more familiar with evidence-based insights will help them become more sophisticated customers who will appreciate the value of more sophisticated solutions, such as Advanced Analytics. This logic holds true at all stages of the data process, whether its improving data quality, where end users will be more precise in data entry if they understand the impact that erroneous and missing data will have later on in the value chain; through to, solution design, where the better end-users understand statistical analysis, the more readily they will engage with solutions that contain predictive modelling. Incubating a learning culture around data related activities will only produce dividends for organisations wishing to develop their capabilities and move forward along the data maturity curve.

Finding the correct pace for change and the right elements within the Data Strategy to move forward with at the right time, is a balancing act. As previously discussed, the value add is a key driver, but success will not come if everything is done at the same time. A logical sequence of advancement is needed. Choosing all new technologies that require hard to find skills will limit your organisation's chance to success regardless of how value-adding they are. Evolving technology and skill development can be slow and needs to be balanced with radical step changes in a number of key areas.

When thinking of radical step changes, if your organisation is located in a relatively remote part of the world, the ability to attract technically qualified and experienced staff is likely to be more difficult than if you are located in a major global city. This may mean you will become more reliant on more expensive staff and third-party options than you had initially envisaged. Careful consideration around each technology choice is needed to ensure that the people aspects are fully understood, not just for the initial deployment but across its technology lifespan.

DATA STRATEGY – SELLING THE VALUE

Some organisations embrace the use of third parties more than building their own in-house capabilities. In one case of a national Hospitality chain, it has made the conscious decision to use expert agencies to support it in managing its marketing activity and its customer communications. This makes sense from the perspective of marketing expertise: the agency has more experience of developing successful targeted campaigns than the relatively small in-house Marketing team, but when it comes to data, who should build and operate the 'campaign engine' is far less clear. Should customer insight and the expertise to understand customer behaviour be outsourced? It is a fundamental business question around what the business mission is. Is the business mission to successfully manage the investment in restaurant bricks and mortar – effectively a real estate business – or is the business mission to deliver customer hospitality – providing homely sustenance away from home? If it's the latter, the ability to understand and target different offers to customer segments is likely to be perceived as more of a core competence and therefore one of the areas in which in-house resources need to be invested in order to grow its capability over time. If the former, then it can be argued that the core competence is about managing the physical asset and the capabilities that support this understanding are the priorities for the in-house teams.

These complex choices need to be embraced by the Data Strategy. A Data Strategy supports the organisation's strategic mission, helping it to leverage data assets in alignment with that mission. Many organisations have started to nominate a Chief Data Officer (CDO) to own that responsibility at a leadership or Board level. This is important recognition within the organisation that data is an asset and it, alongside the data related activities within the business, need to be managed correctly. The appointment of a senior leader to champion and effectively manage data can only help drive formulation and implementation of Data Strategy.

When selecting a CDO, some organisations are investing in a full-time data professional to spearhead their Data Strategy, others are nominating an existing leader within the organisation to take on these additional responsibilities, such as Finance Director or Chief Technical Officer. This later approach is typically less effective and results in a slower paced Data Strategy deployment. Dual responsibilities make for mixed priorities. Somebody who has developed their career within the data profession is more likely to deliver the step change needed to implement a new Data Strategy with vigour.

Publishing the approved Data Strategy across the organisation also helps publicise commitments, highlights responsibilities and communicates the value of the changes ahead. Setting expectations among stakeholders for what will happen not just on the easy to accept aspects of the Data Strategy but also in terms of some of the more difficult aspects, for example around governance of Master Data and Data Security, will be helped by a clear articulation of leadership decisions. Implementing a Data Strategy that has the clear approval of an organisation's leadership is easier than one that is a hidden or secret agenda. When the Data Strategy impacts existing ways of working, visibility and clarity of objectives will help change staff behaviours and secure their buy-in to change.

Target Operating Model

In the world of Strategy Consulting there is a well known saying that 'Structure follows Strategy'[1]. This refers to the fact that only once a Strategy is defined, should consideration be given to its implementation. It also refers in a cautionary way that any organisational structures that are established should be made while keeping the Strategy front of mind. In the same way, once a Data Strategy is defined consideration is needed about the Target Operating Model (TOM) that will enable its successful implementation.

It may be that all the organisational structures needed are already in place. There may also be gaps. We will describe in this book some of the key organisation structures needed for a Data Strategy to become well governed (See Chapter 6). As we have already described above in this Chapter, there are a number of key roles and responsibilities that are needed among staff working with data and on data related activities. Ultimately people need to be incorporated into the organisational structures to ensure that ways of working will be efficient and effective.

Some organisational structures can be maintained as virtual organisations in some situations and in others they are better established

---

[1] Source: Chandler, A.D. *Strategy and Structure*, 1962, The MIT Press, Cambridge (USA)

as a formal unit. For example, Communities of Practice or Centres of Excellence (CoE) do not necessarily need to always be items listed on an organisational chart, instead they could be more informal groupings coming together as needed to share learning and build better practices. The choice will depend on the degree of maturity needed around their remit: such as, is there a large body of work that will need to be managed carefully around a CoE for Analytics, Applications or BI? If the answer is yes, there is a large body of work to be achieved, then typically it is better to establish a formal organisational unit with a responsible CoE Lead.

Similarly, when considering the Target Operating Model, it is important to also get into the detail around ways of working within each organisational structure. Different processes that enable successful delivery will need to be defined and these are discussed further in Chapter 7. Whichever delivery processes are put in place, they do need effective management. The Roles and Responsibilities of Data Staff need to reflect a clear ownership of processes and reporting lines within the TOM.

How to quantify the value of People related activities?

The most common benefit of people related activities is a reduction in time needed to carry out the activity and which, when added across process steps and over longer time periods, combines to enable a full-time-equivalent (FTE) head count reduction. These FTE reductions when multiplied by relevant staff costs (salaries, pensions, social costs, etc.) add up to a certain financial sum which is a saving in labour cost that can either be used to free-up these resources to work on other activities or, if volumes can be increased through the existing process, to increase productivity of the resources carrying out the existing activity or, alternatively, let go from the organisation.

When it comes to FTE reductions, these are of course sensitive employment matters related to individuals' careers and organisations human resource policies. The realisation of anticipated benefits is not the same as quantification of the benefits. What to do with the extra capacity gained from improving a people related activity is open to a wide range of possibilities and only one option would be the severance of the FTE from the organisation. Likewise, an awareness is needed that fractions of FTE are not necessarily a realisable benefit: for example, a 60% FTE reduction, still requires 40% of that FTE.

Other people-benefits that can be defined often relate to capability improvements. Capability improvements, such as new skills, improved competences, acquired certifications, etc. are enablers that allow the organisation to move along the maturity curve. These should be defined and listed in benefits gained, however it is not usual to put a financial value quantification of these benefits. Instead, these capability benefits are typically listed alongside the financial values added from the implementation of the individual use cases of data related activities, so that they are just as visible as the financial gains. Clearly, intangible benefits that are re-usable capability gains should be deemed more beneficial than one off capability gains.

It is helpful to distinguish between real people related benefits and other benefits that are in fact related to new and or improved ways of working, processes and governance mechanisms. More on these in the following Chapters. People benefits however, need to be linked back to specifically identified individuals.

Security needs to be considered throughout People related activities

Appropriate controls need to be followed so that the right people use data and its related data solutions in the right ways. Staff need to be empowered in their data related activities, but at the same time need to conduct themselves in ways that adhere to data security.

Access rights to data may need to be restricted. In many cases, sensitive commercial information may need to be locked, access to personal employee or customer data may need to be restricted, national security data may need to be protected, and so forth. In these cases, data receives a classification and access rights are managed based on the type of classification and related restriction. Similarly, access to whole systems and technologies may be restricted. In simple terms, the fewer people with access rights, the lower the risk of any breaches. Assuming access is permitted, the use of data may then be restricted in certain ways, for example, not to be recorded or printed or disseminated without certain rules and procedures being followed.

To facilitate people working within these secure classifications, individuals can become approved. Approval can be as simple as adding named individuals to a controlled list through to those people receiving specific training related to the restrictions imposed. And, when people no longer need access to data or systems, their user rights should be disabled or withdrawn.

Less formal restrictions in the form of standards and policies however are more widely found. So, for example, how patient data can be used in research will need to adhere to the documented rules. Training of staff in the correct use of data is another way to communicate and reinforce good security practices. Reducing human error through training should increase awareness of security issues, help reduce the number of security breaches and contribute to building a culture that treats data as a valuable asset.

Analysis of user behaviour, particular high-risk users, plays an important part in ensuring the effective security of data related activities. Modifications to data sets should be tracked to identify unusual practices or users. Data Audits can be used to periodically check correct usage and identify any breaches. Sometimes even simple alerts to track the number of log-on attempts to data sets or systems can provide early warnings of potential cyber-attack.

Case Study: Best practice organisational structures in Banking

A well-known global bank asked me what is the best organisational structure to enable its Data Strategy? It is a great question, but rather simplistic if a pre-canned solution is the expected answer. To answer the bank I explained, as we have already discussed above, an organisation's Business Strategy and approach to the market will have a significant impact on the Data Strategy, including the supporting organisational structures that deliver on the strategy. I commented that, adding to the complexity is the fact that the different technology choices made by the organisation, historically and in the future, require different capabilities to be developed and some of these capabilities are best managed in different ways than others. And linked to this, as discussed in Chapter 3, where the organisation is in terms of data maturity also plays an important role in shaping the best delivery structures.

Banks today, like many other long-established organisations, have complex business structures and ways of working. They certainly also have complex business needs. This means a decision such as whether to establish central teams responsible for aspects of delivery will need to vary from case to case. While there are efficiencies to be gained from developing these 'engine rooms' of people to work quickly and leverage scale economies, sometimes the subject matter expertise needed may mean a more 'local' business focused team could be a more effective alternative.

Nevertheless, while a generic 'one size fits all' answer is not possible, typically some quick win benefits can be gained and are relevant to the bank:

> The building of **Competency Centres** or Centres of Excellence for specific domains of activity are highly valuable structural building block for all organisations. A Business Intelligence Competency Centre and an Analytics Centre of Excellence are both great examples in how best to incubate improved practices in their domains. In bringing together members in these Centres, scale and expertise can also be developed and through scale greater efficiency can be delivered.

> Developing **Communities of Practice** of like-interested staff is another structural building block appropriate for all organisations. Communities may be established around specific technologies or practices. For example, a Tableau User Community or a Data Architects Group are really valuable communities to be established to share best practice, enable innovation and support training.

When implementing these structures, I stressed to the bank that both Competency Centres and Communities of Practice can be virtual structures if preferred: they do not necessarily need to figure in organisational charts and hierarchies to be effective. The degree of formality or informality in their structures can be flexed based on the organisational culture and the degree of confidence needed in achieving outputs from them.

In the case of this global bank that asked me its question, the use of both of Competency Centres and Communities of Practice was particularly valuable as they were able to leverage scale economies in delivery from across their worldwide operation. Development best practices in one area of the business could be shared and resources could be deployed using agile work methods across workloads contributing to faster project delivery.

These innovative processes, as we will discuss in Chapter 7, when embedded within new structures like the above are a particularly powerful combination. The adoption of DataOps helped reduce cycle times, processing costs and improved quality levels: all highly valuable in any structure.

CHAPTER 6: Finding the right level of Governance

The degree of formal versus informal governance is at the heart of the culture and ways of working within an organisation. There is not necessarily a right way or wrong way when it comes to the formality of governance systems as both informal and formal approaches can be made to work successfully. The difference is that the informal approach requires much more conversation and continuous re-alignment to maintain appropriate standards. Whereas a more formal approach sets out the standards with the expectation that staff will be monitored and self-govern themselves in maintaining appropriate standards.

Governance practices need to be appropriate to the data related activity being governed. For a senior leadership team dashboard or report, the structure and content may be so important that a very formal governance system around it may need to be applied. This might include defining clear ownership responsibilities for the report, security requirements around the data it draws on, definition of access controls and user permissions, and definition of standards around metrics, content, data refresh schedules and even style of presentation. In another data related activity, a more informal approach is likely to be more appropriate. For example, among a team of data scientists, aspects of data ownership and security can usually be replaced by stewardship. This is because they are data specialists, who as experienced and skilled data users can be trusted to not delete or modify data sets and follow agreed protocols, so some governance elements can be relaxed for the team.

The Data Strategy needs to set out governance plans for data related activities. It will establish areas requiring high levels of formal governance, such as around legal and regulatory requirements, as well as informal approaches, including among other, opportunities for team members to share best practice. With the concept of formal versus informal governance in mind, the frequency of review of any governed system will need to be modified accordingly. This review process should not only look at whether the governance is being followed but also whether the governance system itself is sufficient.

When implemented correctly, good governance systems enable efficiency and speed. They define successful delivery processes to be adopted, including what can be automated, what needs to be enabled to allow self-service, what will require manual intervention and what the intervention process should be. They also enable better quality data sets and help build a 'right first time' mentality, thereby reducing the need for re-work.

Governance of your Data Strategy itself

The Data Strategy describes how data related activities will transform data resources into value for the organisation. This transformation process requires governance to provide visibility and assurance that value is being delivered as planned. Performance milestones need to be identified and measured against across the Data Strategy Roadmap. Key performance indicators (KPIs) can be defined and used to track activities are on track. These KPIs and milestones should be reported on a regular basis to relevant stakeholders.

Where reporting identifies that progress is diverging from plan, a Data Strategy Review Board (see below for further details) should introduce mitigating actions. At the least, lessons learned should be captured so that future plans can be improved. More proactively however, alternative actions should be defined and implemented to bring the Data Strategy back on track or revised.

A Data Strategy should be reviewed on a quarterly basis and updated on an annual basis so that it remains current. As the organisations data maturity moves forward and as data related activities are implemented, the next initiatives should be identified to evolve the strategy. To add these next items to the revised Roadmap, the same process should be followed as was used to define the initial Data Strategy identifying quick wins, radical change and incremental improvement.

Governance of your data related activities

Whether or not your organisation nominates a CDO to own the Data Strategy, some form of top-down leadership will be needed. Individual data related projects and programmes will require management. Data sources will require Data Owners. Data Stewards will need to provide guidance and management of the transformation process.

Internally, new organisational structures will also be typically needed to enable effective delivery of the Data Strategy. Depending on the size of your organisations, key organisational structures to be established include:

1. **Data Strategy Review Board** – the leadership committee responsible for overseeing and approving all data related activities underway in the organisation. The Data Strategy Review Board is typically Chaired by the Chief Data Officer or Senior Leadership Team member and receives representation from the below organisational committees and communities. These representatives raise data related topics for agreement / funding requests as well as sanction.

2. **Data Governance Council** – an internal committee set-up with remit to improve and govern data standards across the organisation. Its role covers the: improvement of data quality and master / reference data, approving new or changed data related processes and ensuring data security. The Data Governance Council manages data related governance responsibilities, such as: nominating Data Owners, Data Stewards, etc., and ensuring that responsibilities are acted on. It also monitors target operating model, data architecture and solution architecture practices to ensure their long-term viability.

3. **Roadmap Programme Board** – an internal committee made up of relevant data owners, data stewards and end-users wishing to start data related projects or report on the progress of live projects. Its role covers the management of the implementation of the Data Strategy Roadmap, where each newly proposed data related project proposal is reviewed, prioritised, approved and or rejected, as well as managed through its project lifetime to ensure objectives and value is achieved. It balances business need against technical, data and planning dependencies in order to rank priorities. It provides visibility of benefits achieved, future dependencies and evolving planning assumptions.

4. **Centre of Excellence for Data, Insights & Analytics** – an internal community made up of data related experts, super-users and, where appropriate, delivery partners who come together to share best practice, raise data related issues, problem solve and incubate innovation. The Centre of Excellence may establish relevant expert or super-user groups on specific topics and technologies, such as around Business Intelligence or Advanced Analytics. This community typically drives the data related training agenda across the organisation. A central co-ordination function of the Centre of Excellence ensures that changes to data related assets are reviewed, approved and communicated to impacted stakeholders. It aims to promote a sense of common ownership in an ethical data culture, where collectively, standards, business logic, KPIs and metrics, ways of working, etc. are agreed to and efforts to have these adopted across the organisation is pursued.

5. **Design Authority** – an internal committee made up of relevant Architects and experts who come together to review and approve data related architectures within the organisation. The Design Authority is responsible for ensuring that any new data and/or solution architecture is fit for purpose and that any new components fit with existing components and ways of working. In so doing designs need to align with the objectives and benefits defined in the Data Strategy. The Design Authority will typically check that any planned and delivered work also aligns with architectural best practices, such as DCAM, Dmbok, TOGAF, etc.

    > **DCAM** (Data Management Capability Assessment Model) is a relatively young but influential framework established by EDM Council members with a particularly strong take-up in the Financial Services arena.
    > **Dmbok** is DAMA International's Data Management Book of Knowledge and one of the oldest and so widely known / used frameworks.
    > **TOGAF** is The Open Group's Architecture Framework: an open and vendor neutral methodology that focuses on Enterprise Architecture standards, including data, application and technology architecture.

Smaller organisations will not need to establish all of the above organisational structures, but if structures are not created, then the responsibilities carried out by the structures will still need to be assigned to relevant individual people or teams. The work these structures are responsible for still needs to be done.

The establishment of the above organisation structures and the correct delivery of their responsibilities is to enable the appropriate governance of data related capabilities through the definition and management of policies, responsibilities and standards. In so doing data related capabilities will also become better enabled through training, wider engagement and communication. As seen in Figure 6 below, governance from this perspective becomes an enabler of continuous improvement.

Through a process of continuous improvement, the business-as-usual activities of: i. defining requirements for minor changes and identifying whole new data related activities for potential release, ii. managing the Roadmap as a Programme or as a set of individual Projects and iii. providing the necessary support Services for existing solutions, as described in Figure 6, are governed through the effective delivery of enabling capabilities. These capabilities cover foremost: the task of ensuring that the people involved in business-as-usual operations have the necessary skills to do their jobs well and, where needed, they receive training to up-skill their capabilities. Additionally, the team members need to understand what their roles are and what the business objectives are to enable successful delivery. Underpinning these fundamental enabling capabilities, the governance role is to set expectations through policies and standards so that the responsibilities are clearly defined for all involved. Once expectations are set, the governance role is also to ensure that expectations are carried through and the defined approach is adhered to.

In smaller organisations, for example start-ups or smaller scale administrations in the public sector, where they don't have the size to warrant establishing organisational structures responsible for the above activities, the use of Figure 6 is particularly helpful to ask the question: who is responsible for these activities? Just as Prince 2 is a valuable method for all organisations working with Projects, so too should a Data Governance approach be established that ensures that data and data related activities are managed effectively by all team members. A formal organisational unit may not be needed, but responsibility for the role and decisions in that domain do need to be assigned to someone.

Figure 6: The Continuous Improvement Cycle

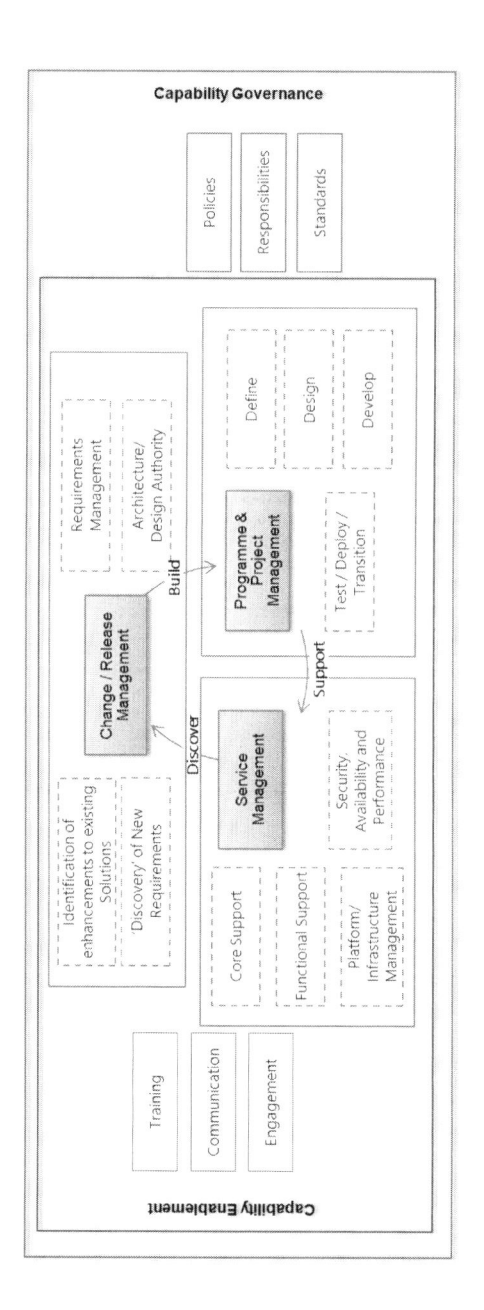

Governance enables and requires effective communication

Improved governance of data related activities should de-risk delivery and should therefore help to improve the chances of success. Over time, as the objectives of the Data Strategy and Roadmap are achieved, more and more successes can be celebrated and news of these successes communicated.

Through greater visibility of Roadmap delivery progress, stakeholders can see improvements happening and they can see what is coming next. Through holding regular gatherings among subject matter experts and super-users, news of smaller locally focused data related initiatives and successes can also be shared with colleagues. Common issues and concerns can also be raised at these gatherings with a view to identifying learnings and solutions that can be shared.

The frequency of communication can be used to build a sense of momentum and dynamism around the Data Strategy, providing in turn motivation to all involved. In particular, when it comes to new data related processes and technical innovation, communication should build a sense of engagement and excitement within the organisations as new benefits are delivered.

Communication however is not just limited to providing news of success: communications also need to be made around ways of working and quality standards. These are perhaps less exciting, but just as important. Those responsible for their areas of governance need to make staff aware of changes and improvements needed. The good news is that if people have seen improvements already being delivered and they understand the rationale for the change, they are more likely to change their existing practices and adopt new approaches.

How to quantify the value of Governance related activities

The benefit of improved governance can be one of the more difficult areas to quantify. Some aspects however are highly compelling. If a specific data related activity has a legal or regulatory requirement around it the penalties of non-compliance are highly visible. Non-compliance may mean a fine or legal action is the result and, in some cases, even a prison sentence may be the end result.

Other aspects are likely to be about de-risking activities. For example, by following the governance standards when conducting reporting, end-users can rely on the outputs and decisions will be based on appropriate evidence. The size of the benefit in this case may be best valued in comparison to the existing practices. What has been the impact of past decisions based on inaccurate data or poorly executed processes? How much money was lost in executing incorrect decisions or time wasted in pursuing erroneous insights? How much time has been wasted for not having agreed definitions for metrics and KPIs?

Continuing with the above reporting example, a study could also be undertaken to quantify baseline performance in terms of time and cost as well as what the introduction of governance improvements would mean to future performance. Such before and after studies provide direct evidence of the quantifiable benefit of any change.

Other metrics used to measure the success of governance activities include:

- **Lead time:** measured as the length of time it takes from starting work on an initiative to deploying it to customers.
- **Recovery time:** defined as the length of time it takes to recover and resolve an issue when it goes wrong.
- **Success rate:** calculated as the percentage of changes made that are successfully made first time.

Security needs to be considered throughout Governance related activities

Governance practices will need to reflect the need for security. Security is a fundamental aspect of Governance and systems need to be governed in ways that secures their correct function. As described above, the degree of control exercised across people, data, processes and technologies will to a large extent depend on the need to secure correct functioning. Legal, regulatory, sensitive and mission critical aspects will require more security and less critical areas normally will require less security.

As the Data Strategy is defined and implemented the Data Governance Council will need to review security on an on-going basis to ensure that governance remains adequate and data related activities are securely protected. A baseline Security Assessment is typically the starting point to assess risks, which can then be revisited on a regular basis. The degree of confidentiality, integrity and availability of data needs to be assessed. All new initiatives coming to the Data Governance Council for approval should be required to address security, where any potential risks and what mitigating actions are needed are clearly identified. The Data Governance Council should also ensure that regular tests are done on security aspects to ensure that these are working and sufficient. The Data Security Assessment should be refreshed on an annual basis, a schedule of data-source audits need to be carried out on a repeating on-going basis, user behaviours need to be monitored and access privileges need to be managed on a systematic basis. The Data Governance Council effectively needs to govern that the security governance is happening!

Case Study: Governance in the Nuclear sector

As a sector one of the most secure and most formally governed has to be the nuclear industry. The ramifications of potential breaches in governance in this sector could literally be lethal. For those not having worked in nuclear energy, governance practices can at first be seen as over-engineered and unnecessarily formal, quickly however the realisation dawns that these efforts are for the safety of everyone: employee, supplier, customer and citizen.

The use of nuclear energy starts with the design and construction of the power station itself. Every aspect of the design and every version of that design has to be approved by the Construction Design Authority and Nuclear Regulator. The requirements for the document management systems alone are some of the most complex imagined. The building of any single nuclear energy site instantly becomes one of the largest and most expensive construction projects undertaken anywhere globally. Every component in the design needs to adhere to relevant quality standards and its source of supply needs to be documented, including in some cases the raw materials used to make the component. All of this information will need to be stored and backed-up, so that it is available as required at any point in the lifecycle of the site. In the case of a nuclear power station the lifecycle is typically 100 years.

Site construction works follows in similar detailed, governed and recorded ways. Not only does the level of risk in each activity need to be tracked, but so do the enormous costs being spent – at Hinkley Point C (HPC) in the south west of England, the construction is anticipated to cost around £25 billion – and the timelines across this highly complex project need to be closely monitored. Any slippage in one area, can have huge cascade effects elsewhere in the programme and costs can quickly spiral upward.

Once built, the power station is typically anticipated to operate for over 20-30 years and governance of its safe operation and supply is paramount. At the end of operation, decommissioning then follows (over a period of some 70 years) where again risk, cost and time need to be continuously monitored.

Robust data management is invaluable when working in such large scale and sensitive activities: having clear naming conventions, defined master data, comprehensive metadata, well architected data stores, good quality data, secure and visible data lineage, etc. all make the consumption of data reliable. If these are not thought through upfront, later changes can be extremely time consuming and expensive.

The Data Governance Council in a nuclear power operator takes ownership and ultimate responsibility for the data related activities across the lifecycle of the site. Its decisions today having ramifications for us all in many years time. This makes time to insight and quality of that insight key. Alongside this on-going governance, a clear delivery Roadmap identifies the data related activities of the operator and its implementation is managed through the Roadmap Prioritisation Committee, made up of senior cross-business leaders, and the Data Architecture Design Authority, made up of Architects and data related subject matter experts.

CHAPTER 7: Adapt processes to work well in your organisation

The successful implementation of Data Strategy requires delivery processes to be effective. Whether new processes or existing processes, all processes need to operate smoothly to enable data to be transformed into value.

Once an effective data related process is in place, the process can be re-used in other areas and a standard process is born. Standard processes equip staff with tried and tested methods that are known to work and allow staff to become efficient in their operation. The alternative would be for staff to be perpetually discovering as they go, one off delivery methods. Time spent building standard processes and refining them to be as effective and efficient as possible pays dividends and allows for the potential value from data related activities to be multiplied.

Data related processes once defined can generally be improved. Once an efficiency level is known, focused interventions can be made to improve on it. Just as data is at the heart of business process re-engineering and Lean methodology, so can the thinking from business process re-engineering and Lean be applied to all data related activities. In so doing, processes are not left to become set in stone, but reviewed, improved and made more relevant.

Many data related processes are simple, others are far more elaborate affairs. When thinking about improving existing processes or implementing new processes, learning from your peers is a sensible approach. Technology vendors will have clear guidance on best practice ways of working with their tooling, other organisations may have experience of the process you are looking at and best practice benchmarks may even exist. Maintaining a watch and willingness to adapt will ensure processes are kept efficient and effective.

Review your existing data related processes

The first step in undergoing any potential process change is to review what is happening currently. In doing this review, hopefully some good aspects will be discovered, but also there are likely to be some areas of poor performance, some overlooked gaps and a level of output that is not as good as it could be.

It is important to define measures of performance across the process, so that the existing process can be adequately judged and any subsequent changes also have a base line against which improvements can be quantified. Measures may include: time, cost, quality levels, as well as certain outputs. When looking across the process certain communication steps may also be involved, for example sending notifications or requesting approvals to managers. In the redesign of the process, it is useful to reconsider if any of these communication steps can be automated or safely removed. Perhaps the use of new additional KPIs and reports will make some communications superfluous?

In your review of current processes, it is helpful to compare these to best practices where possible. Perhaps even a brief benchmarking exercise may be possible to be carried out to help shed light on where existing performances could be improved. Many opportunities for process benchmarking exist, such as the ITIL framework (formerly Information Technology Infrastructure Library) in the Service Management domain, which provides a set of best practice guidance around service strategy, design, transition, operation and continuous service improvement that can be used for comparison and learning. Alternatively, comparisons contained within Maturity Assessments may also provide relevant input.

Once a new process is designed, it is important to test it to see if the anticipated improvements are delivered. At this stage some refinements can also be incorporated until a satisfactory new process is defined. Once the design is finalised, it is tempting to stop and think the job is done. Not quite! There are two more important steps to be followed. Firstly, the new process should be documented, so that new staff to the process have a clear guide to follow and also so that others, elsewhere in the organisation interested in adopting similar processes or those coming back at some future date to review this process, have the current state documentation ready to use. Depending on the complexity of the new process, this documentation may be sufficient alone for staff members to pick-up and implement the new ways of working. In some cases however, additional training materials and, if radically different, entire training programmes may also be needed for impacted staff members. The second step is to communicate to relevant stakeholders about the introduction of the new process, using the new documentation and setting out, with evidence of before and after the process re-engineering, what improvement benefits have been achieved. This last step is particularly helpful. Communicating benefits should help staff involved in the process engage positively with the changes required in the process and so help adoption of the new process.

Roles and responsibilities in data related processes

Perhaps at this stage it is useful to step back and remind ourselves that organisations are built around people and therefore the need for a people centred approach to organisational processes is important. This is also the case for data related activities and processes.

When it comes to data related processes, we need to clearly identify the roles and responsibilities of the participants. We can define participation by answering a series of questions:

1) Who governs the process?
2) Who uses the outcomes of the process?
3) Who works on each task in sequence along the process flow?
4) Who maintains the technology deployed in the process?
5) Who reports on progress and performance of the process?
6) Who innovates the process?
7) Who trains staff involved in the process?

Understanding who are the people and, next question, what are their roles and responsibilities across the process flow, will help staff to be efficient in their work and in their hand-offs to other process members. The process should be deigned in a way that is efficient and effective for the people involved.

No-people processes

Not all data related processes are delivered by people: some are purely automated data flows involving technology. Nevertheless, people are likely to be involved in some way and the above questions regarding roles and responsibilities remain pertinent. For example, in a bank, data ingestion may be automated from an operational trading system to a financial reporting system so that each customer transaction is accounted for and recorded appropriately. Even though this is an automated process however, it is still important to ensure there is a visible record about who governs the process, who uses the outcomes, who maintains the technology used in the process and who checks that the process has been carried out successfully.

Where people have not worked on specific tasks in any way, it is even more important that the details of the task is fully documented, so that there is clear accountability for the work being done. In the above banking example, what transformations are being made to the operational trading data need to be clearly defined. All relevant details about how the transactions are being converted to a single currency before they are transmitted to the financial reporting system and that a time stamp is being applied to the transaction alongside a location description being added need to be recorded. The need for complete documentation around an automated technology process becomes even more important than a process fully carried out by people as often the authors of the automated process flow may have long departed your organisation.

All data related processes require careful documentation. Writing down what is happening in data related processes allows for those involved to understand their roles, but it also allows for interested parties looking to use the data or to apply the process elsewhere to be fully aware of what they are using. Effectively, documentation enables trust across the data flow and allows for the process to be deemed trustworthy. This concept of trust is at the heart of blockchain technology: where blockchain enables distributed trust across each link in the chain. As a result of this trust, blockchain technology is able to rely on processes across multiple organisations. Allowing each organisation in the chain to trust in the process.

Data etiquette

As organisations embrace more and more analytics in their operations, the need for a common understanding of how data should be captured, stored, handled and consumed is increasing. Adhering to a set of legal and regulatory rules is one thing, but often a commonly agreed set of ethics also needs to be applied. What is common sense, obvious or preferred by one person may be very different for another. Organisations that are data mature define a set of common data ethics to be adopted by those when engaged in data related activities. These go beyond a set of rules, but also cover guidelines for ways of thinking and working with data. Hence the term data etiquette.

Data etiquette will, for example, remind staff to delete un-needed email history as it risks becoming an unapproved data store about individuals' behaviours and actions. It will guide how data is used within the algorithms and models made by data scientists. It will also ensure certain customer groups are not discriminated against and that all customers are treated the same. It will even remind developers of what colours to apply in Business Intelligence dashboards, so that all users can interact with the insights in the same way, regardless of whether they are colour blind.

Data etiquette is built up over time and sometimes through painful lessons learned from error. It is important however that data etiquette is captured and written down from which others can read and learn. Making a mistake once is perhaps forgivable, but repeated error should not be tolerated. As organisations move along the data maturity curve, capturing learnings and building an appropriate data etiquette is essential.

The organisational structures as described in Chapter 6, including the Data Governance Council, Centres of Excellence and Design Authority, and the people operating within these structures, including Chief Data Officer, Data Owners and Data Stewards, are responsible for shaping an appropriate data etiquette.

Process typology

There are an increasing number of preferred project delivery methodologies in use today. As mentioned in Chapter 1, Agile development is growing in preference at the time of writing to Waterfall development. At the crux of this preference, is the recognition that Agile's incremental delivery practices provide for earlier wins to be delivered to stakeholders.

Similarly, the rise of DevOps and DataOps are bringing positive changes to data related activities. DevOps methodology started in software development where the traditional emphasis on being project driven or at least focused on individual projects, moved instead to be focused on the need for continuous improvement. DevOps embraces a cultural process to improve development activities and, by so doing, develop applications and services faster. It emphasises the roles and responsibilities of DevOps teams to improve responsiveness and speed.

DataOps is an extension of this same thinking across all data related activities. It emphasises data within the development process and the value data brings to an organisation. DataOps establishes new processes that bring data related development closer to the business: either integrated or automated so that business can more swiftly achieve value from data related activities. For example, data silos are removed through establishing common data-lakes or stores, to enable business stakeholders to quickly build insight from a wide range of curated data sources. Similarly, DataOps establishes 'quick win' development programmes for BI and Analytics to enable fast 'discovery to value' for data related activities.

Through Agile, DevOps and DataOps thinking, Data Strategy can be implemented more swiftly, deliver value sooner and can benefit from continuous improvement mechanisms and a positive data culture once initiated.

How to quantify the value of Process related activities?

When thinking about the value of any process improvement, a first key question to ask is: are the costs of the process something we can control? If we can't change factors to better control the process, whether to improve costs or increase benefits, then energies are probably best spent elsewhere until the situation changes and we can have a quantifiable impact. If the scale of the process is the issue holding process improvements back, it may be that tasks within the process could be looked at separately, but in doing so we still need to first ask: would changes to their cost structure still have a meaningful impact when thinking about the whole process? Similarly, a number of different benefits may be achieved when looking across the process improvement, and each of these benefits can be studied separately, but once assessed they still need to be combined into a consolidated view of the whole process improvement.

The more impactful the potential benefit, the more rigorous and detailed a study should be to ensure that the potential improvement is assessed and quantified correctly. These studies can then look at the different options around process improvement, potentially testing different alternatives and refining the optimal improved process to be implemented. Internal process assessments can be compared to and refined against 'ideal' views as described in industry benchmarks and best practice studies. In all cases, potential process improvements need to be judged based on their legal, technical and operational feasibility of implementation alongside the desirability of any change to management.

When thinking about processes it is helpful to be aware of stakeholder's perspectives. Asking stakeholders to provide their view on how processes are carried out gives the 'perceived' view, this can then be contrasted to the real 'observed' view as captured by a study. Observed studies include Day in the Life investigations, where process steps are observed, timed and outputs recorded by independent analysts. Day in the Life studies are particularly powerful at identifying re-work levels, where time is wasted correcting activities. Often these correcting activities are overlooked when perspectives are initially given. It is rare however for processes to be carried out in a 'right first time' fashion. As a result, a large area of potential improvement benefit can be missed and when these benefits from reducing 'rework' are added up over time they can become quite substantial.

In process re-engineering, Lean and Six Sigma experts aim to develop processes that minimise waste of all types, including re-work. The 8 Wastes are described further in the next Chapter. And, they work hard with the team working in the process to adopt standard work methods and follow the 'optimal' process steps in a systematic manner. In so doing they aim to increase 'right first time' and reduce the need for 'rework'.

Assuming the process can be controlled, it should be possible to measure the current costs 'baseline' and identify the value of any process improvement. Clearly then a judgement can be made as to whether the improvement is financially worth the effort of undergoing the change. Remember here, that any change is likely not just to be a one off improvement, but will generate on-going savings over time. The questions are then: i. if the process improvements are introduced will they remain attractive over the foreseeable time period? And ii. is anything likely to change that means these process improvements cannot be achieved? If the answer to these questions is that the improvement has long term viability and there is no external reason why the benefits cannot be achieved, then implementation should proceed. Clearly, the more impactful and greater the value added by achieving the desired end state the better.

Security needs to be considered throughout Process related activities

Processes need to be updated as security considerations evolve. New regulations often have security implications that will need to be implemented across an organisation's data related processes. The discovery of new risks or changes to tolerances toward known risks will require security procedures to be revisited and processes revised accordingly. Likewise, whenever new ways of working are introduced security implications will need to be assessed to ensure that security is assured. To be robust therefore, a regular monitoring process needs to be carried out to check for security vulnerabilities from internal or external sources. Where any vulnerabilities are identified, appropriate remedial actions need to be undertaken.

Security standards and policies should also be reviewed and impacted processes updated on a regular basis to keep pace with the changing environment. This is particularly important in today's increasingly digital world, where the data environment does not necessarily confine itself to traditional organisational boundaries. Instead, data is frequently brought inside and is transmitted beyond organisational boundaries. As a result, all staff need regular reminders that they need to follow security policies in carrying out their different roles in data related activities.

Finally, where needed, accountabilities for security should also be regularly updated to ensure that governance processes can be effectively maintained. All the various data related roles, including Data Owners, Data Stewards and Data Users, should have clearly defined security responsibilities and these need to be kept up-to-date as requirements evolve.

Case Study: Evidence based Manufacturing process management

A cardboard box manufacturer had invested significantly in improving its manufacturing excellence over the years and its adoption of Lean methodology was seen internally as a source of pride. Data from across the production line was used to identify and improve operational efficiency and effectiveness. Similarly, its logistics team believed they were among the best in their field responding to just-in-time demand from their customers. Unfortunately for the senior leadership team, the state of internal business reporting, meant that there was virtually zero visibility of these excellent performances across the business. By the time Business Intelligence reports were put together, any variation in performance was often days old history.

This did not mean that reporting was not done, on the contrary there were sizeable Reporting and Analytics teams in many business departments and there was an elaborate central Operational Control team that worked to bring the various strands of information together to provide senior leaders with insights. The processes however were what they called 'mandrolic': slow and manually laborious to achieve the visibility needed.

To remedy the situation, a new end-to-end reporting solution was designed to automate data capture from manufacturing machines and feed a suite of management dashboards giving clear visibility of actual business performance as it happens. These dashboards were to be accessible remotely and where performances went out of defined tolerances automated alerts were established to inform the relevant manager responsible for that area.

To build the solution, not only was a technical perspective needed, but also a performance management perspective too. Appropriate KPIs had to be defined in a Master Data Management tool that informed the business decisions management needed to make. These KPIs needed in turn to have a series of supporting indicators that allowed management to really understand the drivers of performance, as well as mapping out a clear view of the organisation's use of data in an organisation wide Data Model.

The data used in the indicators had to be extracted from across the cardboard box production line. Real-time inputs were taken from stock control, customer order management, each production line machine, health and safety, quality control and logistics systems. This data was stored in a new Enterprise Data Warehouse and how data was consumed was defined in a new Data Architecture that was efficient and effective for the use cases.

These use cases included dashboards only accessible to Senior Leadership Team members and domain specific dashboards for departmental Managers, as well as 'drillable' reports and analytics for operational teams to use on the line. Key decision making processes were defined for each business area and the data flows needed to feed those decisions with timely data were identified. Alongside these, the 'optimal' hand-offs to the next step in the production value chain were identified so that stock levels were better linked to the customer order book, production was better informed of quality check results and goods-out were more aware of transport availabilities.

Governance processes were also established so that data quality levels for each data set were defined. This ensured degrees of error could be factored into the different levels of reporting. Robust access controls were introduced so that who accessed what could be tracked. Finally, training on the new system tooling was carried out at all levels in the organisations, so that the new reports and analytics could be used appropriately in the various daily, weekly and monthly business meetings taking place across the organisation.

CHAPTER 8: You must deliver incrementally

A Data Strategy is not implemented quickly: it is effectively an on-going journey. As described already in this book, breaking down the Data Strategy into smaller milestones and mapping these in a delivery Roadmap will help secure buy-in from stakeholders.

Big Bang delivery has been shown to so often disappoint or even fail. How many large-scale technology programmes have delivered only for the recipients of the solutions to ask why was this built or complain that what was built is not what they had asked for? How many technology programmes started with great fanfare, only to be cancelled sometimes several years later as reality throws obstacles in their path and stakeholders are left with nothing but bruises?

Instead, Data Strategy should be delivered in a way to deliver incrementally. The mindset for the deployment of data related activities should be about defining early returns while also setting realistic expectations that some of the bigger benefits will come later in the timeframe. Being smart about goal setting, delivering promised value instalments quickly and being responsible in communications to stakeholders should provide a robust basis for successful Data Strategy delivery.

Incremental Value Add

A Data Strategy needs to have a number of initial quick wins defined in its immediate term delivery timeline. These should be relatively small in scale but of clear business benefit, for example to build out some missing Business Intelligence reports and / or conducting some initial Data Science to better predict performances in an area of operations. Regardless of the topic, these initial quick win programmes demonstrate clearly to all stakeholders that the Data Strategy project is underway and, once delivered, that the initial promises hoped for are really going to be achieved.

Alongside the quick wins, the more substantial data related programmes of work can be started. Again, however, these larger projects and programmes need to be broken down into parts so that some tangible early value is delivered within reasonable timeframes. By so doing, stakeholders will be able to see again that delivery is on-track and benefits are coming through.

Only through delivering quick wins and early-stage benefits will stakeholders build confidence in the delivery of the Data Strategy. Stakeholders will start to believe that the Data Strategy is not just a paper exercise, but real changes are being introduced and real value to the organisation is being delivered.

These wins and benefits provide the basis for narrative and communications across the organisation: they enable a focus on Return on Investment and allow for celebration when it is achieved. These wins also help prevent early closure of project activity when costs are being targeted for reduction and investments are being considered for cut. Tracking these benefits is important, as only when looked at in aggregate, do they tend to provide enough ROI to allow for some of the less tangible work to be carried out, for example: preparations around improving data quality or architecture.

Return on Investment can be defined in terms of quantitative or qualitative benefit. Hopefully, there are some obvious financial gains that can be demonstrated, such as cost savings from process efficiencies or improved revenues generated from new go-to-market activities. Sometimes however the definition of tangible benefit can be more challenging. Data quality and process improvements generally will need to be defined in terms of the savings generated from removing or reducing re-work: if data does not need to be manually corrected how much time would be saved and what is the cost of that effort for that period of time? If that process was improved across its flow and manual intervention is now removed or reduced, how many full-time equivalents are freed?

Returns from investing in improving capabilities again should be considered from a time gained perspective. How much time can be freed-up, for example, by moving away from Excel and using a new BI tool instead, or, what are the time savings gained from being able to predict machine downtime using data science? An example Business Case template is shown in Figure 7 below:

Figure 7: Example Business Case Template

Why?	Options?	Costs?	Benefits?	Who?	Risks?	When?
• Why is this initiative needed? • What is the opportunity?	• What are the implementation and / or solution considerations?	• What are the projected whole-life costs?	• What are the anticipated improvements?	• Who are the stakeholders impacted by this initiative?	• What could go wrong and what is the impact if it did?	• What is the schedule and key milestones?

In Lean, there are 8 Wastes that can be useful to refer to when thinking about identifying and quantifying improvements:

1. **Defects** – Products or services that are out of specification that require resources to correct.
2. **Overproduction** – Producing too much of a product before it is needed.
3. **Waiting** – Waiting for the previous step in the process to complete.
4. **Non-utilised Talent** – Employees that are not effectively engaged in the process.
5. **Transportation** – Transporting items or information that is not required to perform the process from one location to another.
6. **Inventory** – Inventory or information that is sitting idle (not being processed).
7. **Motion** – People, information or equipment making unnecessary motion due to workspace layout, ergonomic issues or searching for misplaced items.
8. **Extra Processing** – Performing any activity that is not necessary to produce a functioning product or service.

Identifying the specific type of waste you want to address will help you to articulate the business case for change.

Foundational activities

It is important to remember that not all Data Strategy initiatives are technical solutions: some are people, process and governance related. Typically, in the initial implementation phase of Data Strategy delivery, there will be a need to reinforce aspects of the Target Operating Model, improve elements of the data governance framework, decide how to better execute ways of working in data programmes and / or enhance people capabilities through training. Many of these initiatives will in fact become on-going programmes in their own right and will continue to evolve over time. Some however may be one off initiatives: implemented to address a specific gap. These elements when kick-started at the beginning of Data Strategy implementation are called foundational activities.

Foundational aspects to be considered during early Data Strategy implementation include:

Enterprise Data Architecture: Given that the Roadmap will include a number of new initiatives to be delivered, it will be important to conduct a detailed review of the future Enterprise Data Architecture that will be needed. This review needs to include an assessment of how the existing data architecture will be developed into the new and what existing elements will be retained and what new elements will be required. The amount of change will clearly vary from organisation to organisation, sometimes whole new data platforms will be needed and at other times only minor adaptations will be necessary.

Data Model Definition: In all cases where a new Data Strategy is being implemented it makes sense to develop a clear model of the existing data in the organisation and how it relates to each other. Sometimes a data model will already exist and may only need to be brought up to date, but on other occasions a data model will need to be developed from scratch. Regardless this foundational data modelling work will enable the organisation to better understand existing data, including its type, source and structure. It will also enable better communication between technologists and business people within the organisation about what insights are needed and how data sets are inter-related. This is discussed further in Chapter 10.

Master Data Management: Related to data modelling and the development of an 'efficient' data architecture is master data management. Here, business people and technologists come together to decide what are the core sets of data that need to be managed centrally for the benefit of the whole organisation. This typically includes data such as customer, product, service, departments, teams, locations, regulations, materials, etc. but the exact data will depend on the purpose of the organisation and its mission. Master data will be needed by multiple areas of the organisation and so it makes sense to construct an approach to ensure a single source and version of truth when it comes to its use: helping develop uniformity and accuracy in the data used across the organisation, but also enabling correct management (stewardship and accountability) of the master data.

In addition to the data related activities above, people related foundational work may also need to be implemented as part of the Target Operating Model. This will allow for better people management, improved adoption of processes to be followed and the introduction of new organisational structures that will better enable the successful delivery of the Data Strategy. These aspects were discussed in more detail in Chapter 5.

Data Strategy evolves

As organisations develop so too will their Data Strategy. The most obvious example of where a Data Strategy must evolve given new circumstances is when a new business is acquired and needs to be integrated. Instantly the previous organisation acquires new people, new technologies, new processes, new governance structures and new data resources. All of these will need to be included in a new joined-up and coherent Data Strategy.

At some level, whenever the organisation does something new, even if not at the scale of a new business acquisition, that new action will require a sense-check of the Data Strategy to see if it is still applicable or requires some revision. A good example here is when a new supplier relationship is formed and that supplier provides access to new data, then whole new possibilities may need to be considered for the ingestion, storage, governance and consumption of that data and decisions related to these may mean a revised Data Strategy is needed.

To be kept current your Data Strategy needs to be revised on an annual basis. This annual update provides the opportunity for all stakeholders to be advised on delivery progress and any new objectives that have been added. Communications should focus on the value delivered or the value to be gained and when it will be gained.

Improvements to existing data related activities should also be made incrementally. Degrees of sophistication should increase to improve data maturity across the organisation. This approach will reinforce a learning mindset and continuous improvement culture. Data etiquette should be made visible and practices honed to improve standards. For example, when it comes to data science, the formulation of algorithms should be documented in an algorithm library so that decisions made in its development are clearly exposed. In this way, even in the most innovative areas of data related activity, trust can be established that best practices and appropriate quality standards have been followed in the deployment of Data Strategy solutions.

Data Strategy should still be partly radical

Despite the above commentary that value needs to be delivered incrementally and that a Data Strategy must be allowed to evolve over time, there is still room for a Data Strategy to be radical. A radical move to jump along the data maturity curve and introduce some radically new data related innovation is perfectly compatible. This radical innovation does need to be handled correctly as per the wider Data Strategy Roadmap, but there is no reason for the Data Strategy to be limited to evolutionary changes only.

In most organisations in fact, there is plenty of scope within the Data Strategy to incorporate both incremental and radical initiatives. Clearly resourcing and capabilities need to be sufficient to support both, but the benefits of having radical as well as incremental new activities are powerful.

Radical change becomes a method to jump forward with the organisation's Data Strategy and arrive at new levels of capability in a short time period. How much radical change can be included in the Data Strategy will vary from organisation to organisation, largely dependent on the level of investment the organisation is willing to make. The level of investment needs to be based on the value of the returns the Data Strategy will bring. Typically, the Data Strategy should include a small number of radical data related activities and a larger number of incremental changes. However, the only limiting factor to the potential amount of value generated by Data Strategy is the ambition of the corporate strategy itself.

The need to focus on the value that the radical data related activity will bring still applies. The fact that there may be a significant capability jump from what happens today in the organisation to what would be needed to successfully implement this step change, implies an increase in risk that will need to be managed carefully. Appropriate governance around this area of radical innovation will be needed to report on and manage its successful implementation. New skills and potentially new people to implement the innovation will need to be acquired. New processes within which these people operate will need to be established. And lastly, as we have discussed, appropriate technology to deliver the innovation will need to be furnished.

Case Study: Customer facing solution development in the Road Transport Sector

A market leading vehicle leasing business recognised that it needed to better exploit its commercial use of data to build business value. It decided it wanted to focus on digital innovation in areas that would support its business growth. Having reviewed a number of options: it identified an area to build a proof of concept (POC) that is believed would add value for its customers. The POC would test the feasibility of delivering automated insights to fleet operators on the whereabouts and availability of fleet vehicles. In the first instance, the initial POC would be built for use internally by its own vehicle leasing fleet managers, but if proven acceptable and access to real-time customer vehicle data was granted, it would then be rolled out to its customers' fleet operators.

Initially a relatively simple dashboard application was defined: when a commercial fleet manager needed a temporary replacement vehicle for an out-of-service fleet vehicle, the manager needed to know the cost impact of different vehicle choices. If the replacement vehicle was literally a stop gap for a small number of days, a daily rental hire would likely be more flexible and cost effective, but if the replacement was for a little longer then it is likely a short-term lease would be the more cost-effective option for the customer. To get to these conclusions today, a relatively laborious review and side by side comparison of different files was needed. Instead, the POC would make this instantly available 'at a click' and the different options for each available replacement vehicle would be transparently flagged so the fleet managers could make the best real-time allocation of vehicles. Different types of vehicles could be shown, allowing the user to choose the cheapest or highest specification vehicle as needed.

This POC application was initially built and tested by internal users. Having passed its initial testing, the application was then trialled with a small number of customer fleet operators to check that the anticipated business value add was real. Building on that initial success, a subsequent phase of work was planned to enhance the functionality of the initial application with additional features detailing further running cost information on the vehicles available to include cost of usage for petrol, diesel and electric fleet vehicles. This later extension was seen as particularly important as it aligned with the growing green agenda of many commercial vehicle users.

The longer-term Roadmap would then be to add a number of new related applications and overtime to build a suite of tools for the fleet operators. These covered vehicle maintenance and repair activity; driver behaviour analytics (speed, accident, fuel utilisation, etc.); and, route planning support functionality (optimising fleet route mapping, best fuelling point options, fleet vehicle distribution by region, etc.). In this way a fully integrated suite of applications would be incrementally developed, helping the vehicle leasing operator to better support its customers by providing functionality that it could 'test as it was built' from not just a technical but also a business value perspective, enabling them to partner with their customers, using ever increasing amounts of customer data but equally over time to providing back increasingly valuable insights to improve cost, environmental, driver and journey management activities.

CHAPTER 9: Data is the untapped asset in your organisation

The business potential from the better use of data is finally starting to be realised. Commentators everywhere remind us that: a digital business revolution is underway, a 4th Industrial Revolution has begun, the age of the Internet of Things is upon us, and efforts to seize the Artificial Intelligence and Cyber initiative are in full swing. Certainly, organisations are investing in data related activities more than ever before and those that position their use of data as a differentiator are swiftly becoming the most successful in their field.

The 4th Industrial Revolution

Building on developments from the 1st Industrial Revolution that introduced mechanisation instead of human labour, the 2nd Industrial Revolution that extended the use of technology, drawing on electricity and transportation innovations, and through the 3rd Industrial Revolution that digitalised industry thanks to computer technology. The 4th Industrial Revolution is the on-going automation of industrial manufacturing practices, using modern 'smart' technology approaches. Machine-to-machine communications are improved, manufacturing processes become self-monitoring and smart technology conducts self-supported analytics / diagnostics removing the need for human intervention.

The Internet of Things

The Internet of Things (IoT) describes the connection of physical objects or 'things' to the internet. Devices and systems are embedded with sensors, software and other technologies for the purpose of connecting and exchanging data with other devices and systems over the internet, creating a network or an internet of things. The concept of 'smart' homes, cars, offices, etc. has been developed to describe multiple everyday objects (such as lighting, audio devices, cameras, thermostats, security systems and other appliances) being connected together across the same ecosystem network and being able to be controlled via devices associated with that ecosystem, such as through personal computers, as well as smartphones, smartwatches and smartspeaker devices.

Artificial Intelligence and Cyber Initiatives

The term Artificial Intelligence (AI) is used to describe a system's ability to correctly interpret external data, to learn from such data, and to use those learnings to successfully achieve specific goals and tasks through flexible adaptation. AI often draws on algorithms – effectively a set of instructions to be executed – that can be developed cumulatively and are 'learned' from data. Building on this area, Cyber Initiatives aim to understand and define the function and process of entire systems that have goals and that participate in circular, causal (input-output) chains. Once defined, this understanding can be used to optimally automate systems identifying appropriate actions to take to achieve or get close to achieving the desired goals. A great example of AI is a website Chatbot, that recognises questions and provides learned responses to users. Cybersecurity is a good example of where a range of cyber initiatives are used to address a particular problem: for example, using AI to detect phishing, neural linguistic programming to better detect suspicious content and machine learning to identify unusual patterns of user behaviour.

In today's commercial landscape, Amazon and Google are perhaps the archetype data driven businesses, generating vast revenues across consumer and business-to-business sectors offering compelling market propositions to their customers all enabled through a data driven business model. Leaders in other sectors, from airlines, to taxi companies, to hotel and holiday businesses, to home delivery services and pizza companies are embracing data related business opportunities at the core of their strategy.

Beyond commercial enterprise, data driven operation is just as importantly having its impact. From public transport, national health services, border control to armed forces, every branch of the public sector is reinventing itself to better use data in its mission to better serve its citizen. Freely available data or 'Open Data' to third parties is also being actively released by many public sector organisations (and increasingly some private sectors businesses sectors too). Transport for London is one such organisation that makes some of its operational travel data freely available to users via a unified API to use in their own software and services: including timetable and travel disruption data.

The vast majority of organisations of any type today have started reimagining what they can do with their data assets. Unfortunately for many this has led to a lot of trial and error. Instead, a more robust and systematic approach is needed: starting with a Data Strategy focusing on value.

Strategic intent is needed

Strategic intent is needed to manage the abundant yet often inadequately handled data asset. Strategic intent deliberately sets out the choices made and the priorities to be implemented. Strategic intent will also force a focus on the quantification of the value to be extracted from data related activities. This in turn will allow for activities to be prioritised and a Data Strategy and Roadmap to be developed.

The Data Strategy can then be the mechanism for bringing investment to data related activities. Over time, these initiatives will support their targeted revenue increases or improvements in speed, quality and / or cost. By so doing and as the Data Strategy is implemented, new strategy will emerge and the Roadmap will need to be updated accordingly, as seen in Figure 8 below. Intended strategy is bolstered with emergent strategy on an on-going basis and unrealised strategy is clearly identified. The benefits of realised strategy are also tracked and communicated. Appropriate control processes can also be put in place to inform implementation progress, scan for new potential areas of development and enable the organisation to re-act in a timely way.

Growing recognition for data as an asset

As the number of people in the organisation starting to appreciate the potential value of data grows, so too does the realisation that doing nothing is not a viable option. Many businesses long term viability is being hampered by not managing their data assets correctly and by not developing new propositions based on the better use of data. Business differentiation is being diluted, innovation slowed and staff career progressions are being limited.

Figure 8: Data Strategy Implementation[2]

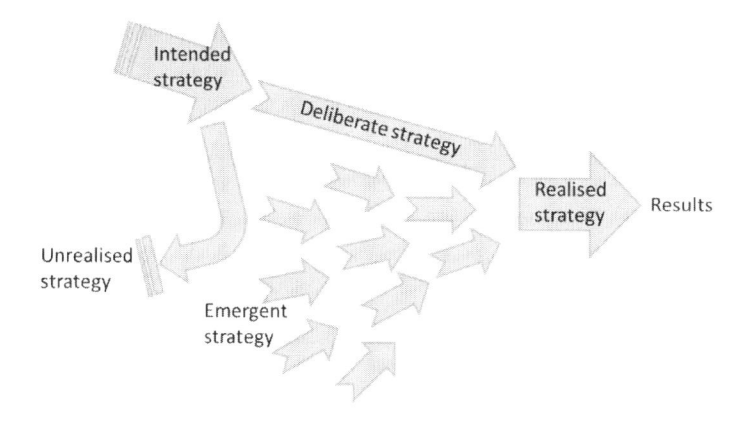

[Figure showing strategy flow: Intended strategy → Deliberate strategy → Realised strategy → Results, with Unrealised strategy branching off and Emergent strategy feeding in]

Data is the critical evidence needed to inform and influence strategy. Data also enables an evidence based culture. Just as there are human resource management practices and financial management practices, so too, data management needs recognition. Data related activities need to be managed in the same professional manner as these other assets. No longer should organisations tolerate 'gut based' decision making instead of 'evidence based' decision making. Poor quality data entry should be tackled and re-work minimised so that data through curation and improvement becomes trusted. More real-time data should be used instead of dated history to keep pace with the speed of change in today's turbulent world. Processes should not be left to trial and error, but standardised and improved. New improved technologies should be deployed to replace antiquated legacy systems that are holding organisations back.

In the past data has been left to the care of siloed Data Owners who while experts in their domains tend to be blinkered by the needs of those domains. As Data Strategy unfolds, increasingly more joined-up thinking will be needed, where data will not just be used by one functional area but will be used across the organisation for the benefit of many. Looking further ahead again, data will also be shared beyond the organisation with suppliers and customers alike. Data will also be combined with external sources, some in open data exchanges and others in

---

[2] Source: Mintzberg, H., Quinn, J. B. and Ghoshal, S. *The Strategy Process (European Edition)*, 1995, Prentice-Hall International (UK) Ltd., Hemel Hempstead

subscription-based libraries, and new extended data value chains will be built for the benefit of all stakeholders across the chain.

As the users of data multiply, the need for good quality, curated and governed data becomes ever more important. Validated data catalogues will be needed to allow users to self-serve. Data lineage will need to become visible, so users understand the origin of and the transformations to data. Metadata will come of age to better describe data assets so that they can be better mined. And, as users of data better understand their datasets, so too will they want to better understand any transformations used in the many outputs and data solutions that are deployed.

As the handling of data becomes ever more sophisticated and professional, so too will the need for the professionalisation of the data handlers grow. Those working in data related activities will need to increasingly be able to demonstrate their capabilities. Certification of acquired skills, proofs of continued professional learning, listed approvals to access and consume curated data sets, memberships of internal and external bodies and participation in data communities will grow in importance.

How to quantify the value of Data related activities

As recognition for data as an asset grows, so too does the need to prioritise and distinguish the value that can be delivered from data usage. The cost of adding new data sets should be relatively transparent in terms of direct purchase costs or data gathering costs. The data handling or processing costs that follow should hopefully also be possible to quantify. The investments needed by these end-to-end data related activities should then be consolidated to form the cost side of the return-on-investment calculation. On the return side, any new advantageous outcome such as tangible revenue generation or intangible performance improvements should be possible to identify. And, the basic assumption is that benefit should be greater than cost.

When it comes to data improvements, typically data related benefits will be best assessed by quantifying the savings from removing re-work. Re-work related to data can be considerable. It starts with incorrect data capture or entry where data may need to be corrected or fully completed to enable its onward utilisation. Then as data is ingested or transferred into data stores additional re-work may be needed, such as the application of metadata to it. Subsequent transformation steps follow the same logic, where the work needed in any transformation step should be quantified, costs calculated and benefits defined.

The above holds true for 'project' related improvement activities, but the cost-benefit of on-going improvement activities are typically not calculated on any regular basis. Instead, costs are incorporated into the running cost of business functions or services. In the case of Centre of Excellence staff, Data Stewards or Architecture teams will typically include any improvement activities as part of their business-as-usual work and the cost-benefit of that work will be factored into staffing budgets and the general availability of these resources to support activities.

In terms of determining the value add of new data solutions and outputs (Analytics, Applications, BI and other Technology Solutions), these are best defined as individual projects or grouped together in delivery programmes with their respective build costs and quantified benefits calculated. It is important to note that not all new solutions are developed by central teams, instead a lot of activity will be generated by business areas and the super-users within those areas. The cost-benefit analysis and investment decision for these works is typically taken within the business area itself. Governance staff however should nevertheless be aware of these activities and be comfortable that it aligns with and is included in the Data Strategy and Roadmap.

In the below Figure, a Business Intelligence and Analytics (BI&A) delivery model is depicted identifying both corporate and functional area fulfilment of the Roadmap activities. Here scheduled Roadmap initiatives are enriched by new innovative BI&A as well as emergent ad-hoc reporting. The flows across the teams are also identified, including the development of requirements, the sharing of capability insights between teams and the making available of team expertise to support delivery. Through close collaboration between the corporate centre and business areas the BI&A Roadmap is delivered.

Figure 9: A centralised and localised Business Intelligence & Analytics delivery model

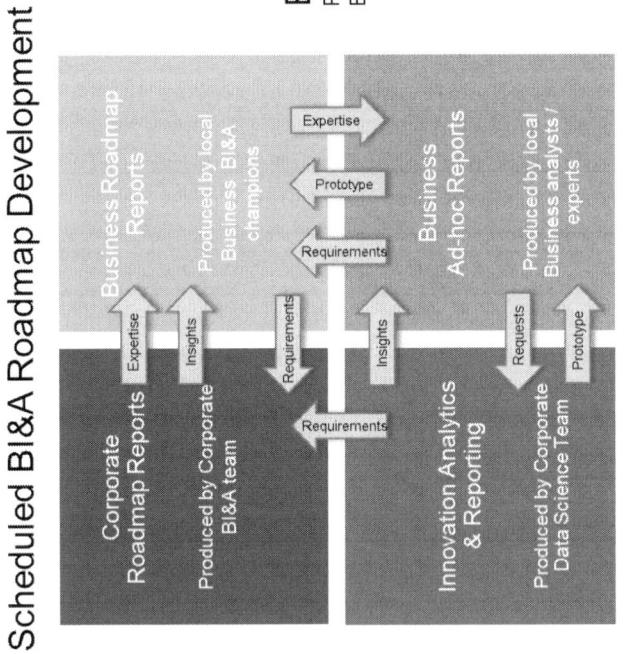

Security needs to be considered throughout Data related activities

Some data sets need to be managed in more secure ways than others. Each data set needs to be assessed for how it should be managed, including consideration for its security. Typically, a classification to data sets is defined, so that data handlers know how to process or consume it in adherence to security protocols. Access rights for sensitive data sets can also be applied so that only those who need access have access. These data confidentiality procedures ensure that data is accessed only by authorised individuals. Knowing who has access to what data is a key security consideration for all organisations. Increasingly today monitoring and real-time alerts on systems and tools are set-up to report on this.

The concepts of data integrity and data availability are key aspects of data quality, which is another enabler of security. Data integrity work aims to ensure that information is reliable as well as accurate. Without data integrity, security cannot be achieved, as information cannot be relied upon, as it is highly likely to be inaccurate. Similarly, data availability is needed to ensure that data is both available and accessible to satisfy business needs. Without data availability, security cannot be achieved, as business needs will be unsatisfied. Data capture, storage and back-up are key processes to ensure data availability. Mission critical and sensitive data capture, storage and back-up processes are the most important to manage effectively.

As organisations become ever more digital, security concerns across all data related activities are increasingly important to get right. Efforts to remove risk, improve efficiency, protect processes and enhance data sets are all key in securing data as an asset.

Case Study: Building new data driven business propositions in Insurance

The insurance sector, like other sectors, is realising the potential business value that can be developed through improved use of data.

In one global insurance business, it has realised that some of its commercial customers would be happy to move beyond the traditional annual renewal model if it made commercial sense. The Insurer realised that they could better use the customer data they had already collected to calculate annual premiums to better address a customer's risk position and in so doing develop a new value-added service that would be less costly for all involved.

Taking the example use case of commercial flood prevention insurance, they could use the same data that is collected to calculate the insurance costs of covering a customer's factory from the risk of flooding and use this data to support the development of a business service that would guarantee that the factory would not be flooded. Here the Insurer would invest in flood prevention measures and take real-time customer and environmental data to track whether the flood conditions were being adequately addressed so that, rather than charging an annual and sometimes highly variable premium to the factory, instead it would charge for a monthly service to prevent flooding.

In this new business model, any risk of flooding becomes covered by the monthly service charge and risk prevention costs around the factory are absorbed by the Insurer themselves. The wins for the insured factory operator are that: (1) monthly service charges will be a little lower than the highly variable annual insurance premiums and (2) the risk of not being able to operate the factory in case of flooding is effectively removed as the Insurer will monitor and take preventative measures on an on-going basis. The wins for the Insurer are: (1) they receive more reliable revenue streams as the insured factory customers are tied-in for a specified period of service and (2) they reduce the risk of having to pay out for commercial losses due to flooding where there have been inadequate preventative measures taken.

This business proposition, however, would only be possible by both the Insurer and the factory customer agreeing to share data. Data that was previously an annual snapshot used to calculate premiums, would now need to be ingested on a minute-by-minute basis and combined with new external data sources, such as local water table data and weather data, to enable a live flood prevention system. By bringing these data sets together and through the development of this new proposition, flood prevention insurance has changed to become a true data driven initiative.

CHAPTER 10: Some data is better than others

All data has some potential to become of value, but it is the use case that determines which data is more valuable than others. To be of value, the different types of data must be captured, stored, cleaned and monetised. We look in this Chapter at some of the considerations needed in how this is best achieved.

Over recent years, there has been exponential growth in the production and availability of data and this shows no sign of stopping. Everything we do from our birth and throughout our lives is now generating data that we and the parties we interact with are consuming for a range of purposes: from selling us goods and services for commercial gain, to monitoring our behaviours and actions to keeping us and our communities safe.

How data is used across those use cases varies greatly. For each use case, the criticality of that data in the value chain will depend on use case circumstances. In this Chapter, we will explore how data is monetised and look at in particular mission critical data.

Data typology

All organisations have the full spectrum of data types within their data environment. Data is hugely varied and includes: numbers, words, sounds, images, tasks, whole processes and measurements (size, weight, temperature, taste, colour, etc.). The variety of data is enormous and new formats continue to be added with the arrival of new technology.

In data programming, data is transformed into numbers (also known as integers), characters and logical values (true or false facts). Data types effectively define what the data programmer can do with the data. Today the use of the full range of data types is increasingly feasible. Hand-written letters can be digitally scanned using Optical Character Recognition software to turn them in to useable format and these text files can be mined for relevant content to be included in business processes. They can then be added to source system data fields, be consumed in reporting or by analytical processes. Images can be scanned using, among other, facial recognition software or fingerprint readers to detect known features and attribute specific identifiers. In other words, helping distinguish between one individual and another. Voice recognition software is regularly used in call centres, to identify variations in voice patterns and word structures, to help detect fraud or monitor customer sentiment. And, through natural language processing methods different data can be collected regardless of the source type on defined themes to build aggregated views. Where, for example, data is taken from verbal quarterly news releases to the market and combined with trading volumetric data to inform insights around trading positions and risk.

In all cases, including those above, data remains raw information until it has gone through a process of classification and analysis. Only once the information has been consumed by a user for a purpose or defined use case does data become a product or insight. Finally, in cognitive terms, it is the understanding and application of insight that then transforms it into knowledge. In terms of maturity journey, solutions using cognitive analytics are the most sophisticated. They take data inputs, interpret those inputs as specific learned insights and draw on those insights to decide appropriate actions. For example, artificial intelligence systems use programmed insights about train timetables along with real-time data on exact locations of trains to manage the availability of platforms at train stations and so support station managers in their decision making to safely and efficiently manage operations.

Data capture

Data is captured in a variety of ways: through human observation and measurement which is then manually entered all the way through to the use of ever increasingly complex mechanisms (from weighing scales, thermometers, speedometers, microphones, cameras to voice recognition, optical character recognition, visual learning, etc.). The arrival of the internet has made the transmission of data far easier than ever before. Data can be distributed in batches, for example over night or on an hourly basis, as needed by the use case requirements. Alternatively, data can be streamed on a nearer to real-time basis and to support this many data capture devices have established ready-to-use Application Programming Interfaces (APIs) within their operating systems that facilitate the transfer of data from a source system to a data store or directly into another application.

As the name implies, real-time data is about the immediacy of data transfer: effectively data is instantly transferred as it is created. In many cases, real-time is often not needed, as long as it is fast. Taking the example of a geo-positioning navigation app, it may be said to receive real-time traffic updates, but in reality, a time lag of a few seconds or minutes exists which is unlikely to concern most drivers. In some cases however, real-time is critically important, so for example, in financial trading the need for immediate data is commercially essential and traders can lose or make significant amounts of money on their ability to transact ahead of others in the market. At one level, it may be fine for a 'casual' investor to buy or sell shares based on a market knowledge using only free available financial website stock market data. This may mean their trade is based on as much as 20 minutes delayed information. Compare this however to 'professional' trading companies. They make huge investments in Direct Market Access to stock market transactional data to enable ever faster trading based on latency times counted in milliseconds. For professional traders, data latency has a completely different meaning!

For other organisations however it is less about data availability and data latency, instead it is about data multiplicity. Rather than extending efforts to capture new sources, effort instead needs to be placed on reducing the number of sources and versions of similar data types. Over the years an organisation procures external data and sometimes this continues to be supplied even when no longer needed, or, without realising, different parts of the organisation procure very similar data feeds separately from each other when one common data feed would be sufficient. Here, the issue is less about not enough and more about needing to understand what is available. It is important to not proliferate inefficiencies, instead focus on building one version of the truth and manage data sources effectively including those that are now legacy (which means sometimes deciding to turn them off!).

Data storage

The purpose of data storage is to remove the risk of not having data available in the future. Implicitly data is given a notion of potential value:

if it were not available, a data related activity or insight would not be possible to achieve.

This does not mean that all data is stored for a known defined purpose, but rather that it is believed that one day the data should be of value to the organisation. In one airline company I have worked with, all the millions of aircraft data points are captured from each of its aeroplanes in its fleet from the moment they are turned on through to the point they are shut down each and every day. All the on-board sensor data produced during each flight is downloaded every day in an ever-growing data store. At present, only a tiny fraction of this data is being consumed by the aircraft operator to drive some operational metrics and used for specific uses, in their case to better schedule maintenance, yet the operator knows there is significantly more potential in the aircraft data, so for now it has decided to store it and wait for the right time to build new use cases.

Typically, data that is stored for a defined purpose will be structured in a way to facilitate that purpose using a data model described below. Data that does not yet have a known use case will typically be stored in unstructured formats as delivered by the source system / author. A good example of this may be historical email data or letters received by an organisation and archived for future use. Prior to their use however a use case would need to be defined and method to extract the specific insights needed from this data would need to be identified. Until then the data remains classified as unstructured.

Where data is physically stored has modified over recent years from on premise 'tin' servers (from Dell, IBM, Intel, etc.) that were managed by internal IT teams to 'cloud' platform services from (Amazon, Google, Microsoft, etc.). Rather than requiring an upfront investment to own disk space and processing the cloud platform business model is to subscribe and pay as you go for storage and processing. Thanks to the internet and the rise of cloud data platform operators, storage has become effectively infinite in capacity and the use of data stores, at least initially, cheaper than ever before. The hardware involved in data storage has effectively become outsourced, along with the need to maintain, manage and secure that hardware. Organisations instead need to focus on when and how to exploit these data sources.

Data models can be helpful in this regard. A data model provides users of data with a method of communication and description of data architecture. There are 3 broad types:

1. The **Conceptual Data Model** defines WHAT data is contained in the system and is typically created by Business stakeholders and Data Architects. The purpose is to optimally organise data, clarify scope and define business concepts and rules.
2. The **Logical Data Model** defines HOW the system should be implemented regardless of the technology to be used and is typically created by Data Architects and Business Analysts. The purpose is to develop a technical map of rules and data structures that apply to the organisation's data.
3. The **Physical Data Model** describes HOW the system will be implemented using the chosen technology and is typically created by database analysts and developers. The purpose is to enable the efficient and effective implementation of the data store itself and support the successful delivery of the end-to-end data platform.

Beware however creating models for the sake of 'beauty' alone: models are useful when being used. If the organisation is not using them and if their revision is slowing down the pace of change in the real world, it is important to revisit the resources needed to manage these effectively and the value they bring.

Data cleaning

In order to be consumed by data solutions to derive the outputs needed, some data may need to be cleaned and corrected. Data cleaning includes measures to correct data quality issues, for example changing dates to be in the same format or modifying data to adhere to naming conventions, classifications or scales. Data may also require completion, for example addresses may be missing some part such as name of Country or postal codes. These cleaning activities will standardise formats so that data can be later processed without error. In other cases, data may need to be excluded as it is of too poor quality, only partially completed or entered as just a test case. A large number of tools exist, drawing on fuzzy logic and machine learning, to help in this data cleaning process to speed up and even automate many of the routines.

The addition of metadata and or contextual data to raw data feeds helps add further value. These additions, such as time stamps, source system references and author identifiers, provide critical context to the data and enable its use to become more effective. The provenance of data, known as data lineage, is increasingly important in many organisations for reasons of compliance, so that each data point can be given appropriate levels of trust. Data lineage tools are particularly valuable in demonstrating and thereby building confidence in data sets as well as speeding up any changes needed in the handling of data as requirements on it change. For example, as a new regulatory requirement comes in to effect, the data identified to have been used in a previous version of the regulation can be quickly identified in a data lineage tool and any new modifications in the use of that data can be made accordingly.

In some organisations, mission critical data is managed in a different way to other data types. Relevant authorities, such as regulators and governments bodies, may dictate that certain data is managed in specific controlled ways. Some apply different standard certifications or labels to data sets based on the degree of confidence that a user can have in their quality. For example, a report describing the performance of a mission critical area of activity, may use only Gold Standard data, where as an ad-hoc report that was quickly put together to show latest data around an activity may use not-yet-signed-off Bronze Standard data.

Data monetisation

Data has the potential to be of value, but as we have seen above, in order for that value to be realised it needs to undergo processing. It needs to be captured, stored, cleansed / prepared, transformed / combined and served up / consumed by tools / solutions. This handling costs money to set-up and carry-out. At the least therefore the value add of data should cover its processing costs. In many cases however data is seen like water, air or light. It is a utility that is simply consumed without much thought. In other cases, it is of course like a rare diamond: to be treated as something precious and used with care. In all cases value can be applied to data.

When data is used to derive tangible benefit, the data is said to be monetised. This may be the value saved from the automation of a process instead of carrying out the process manually. It may be the value gained by introducing a new go to market proposition. It may be the value achieved from mitigating a particular risk. Alternatively, at its most simple, it could be the value added by selling data to another organisation.

Mission critical data

Data that enables organisationally important activities is of high value. The more important the activities are to the mission of the organisation the more value the data has. Mission critical data will be used to inform stakeholders about the key decisions they make, will be incorporated into business propositions for customers, will flow across the business value chain, will enable measurement of past, current and future performance, and so forth. They will be used to better support the organisation in the delivery of its strategy and mission.

A Data Strategy needs to focus foremost on mission critical data and data related activities around it. Activities that optimise the handling and full exploitation of mission critical data should be prioritised above other less important data and supporting activities.

A business impact analysis can be conducted to help determine what is mission critical data. This analysis should be integrated into the on-going Security Risk Assessment programme so that data confidentiality, integrity and availability is securely managed as per its assessment category.

Case Study: Data in the world of Healthcare

Healthcare data is very diverse and yet the data sets are very often of most value when they are inter-related. Healthcare data is also by its nature very often personally sensitive and protocols for its correct handling and access are typically stringent. The value from its correct use however is very high.

In the case of a Patient Level Information and Costing System (PLICS), the full diversity, the inter-related nature and the sensitivity of data is clearly seen. PLICS aims to provide detailed information about the cost of treatment of a patient in a hospital. Literally, the duration and type of care provided for each individual patient's episode in the hospital is captured from entry to Accident and Emergency, through Treatment and Discharge or through Hospital Admission, In-patient treatment and Discharge. Alongside patient outcomes, at each stage of healthcare provision the time taken, names of Medical staff handling the patient, costs of drugs and supplies consumed by the patient, procedures undertaken and locations of stay are tracked. Each of these units of care are costed and attributed to the patient and ultimately an individual cost of care for a specific episode of treatment can be calculated.

How this is achieved however is not straight forward! Data is captured within stand-alone systems across a hospital's Information Technology architecture. Data from these source systems needs to be correctly captured and ingested into a common data record. Costing information then needs to be applied to resources (staff, equipment, drugs and other consumables) as well as to the activity undertaken (time in the different services, number of procedures carried out, tests made, etc.). An individual patient's consumption of resources and activities can then be established and their outcomes, for example, number of days to discharge, can be identified.

In this PLICS case, the value gained is multiple. Each individual siloed data set already has value, for example Accident and Emergency data helps manage the safe and efficient running of that Department. But, when data from across a full patient journey is tracked across multiple Hospital Departments and combined with cost, resource, activity and outcome data the value gained is even greater. True costing information is identified based on resources consumed and activities carried out which can allow for improved cost efficiencies to be found. Patient outcomes can be looked at in context of individual patient journeys which can allow for more effective patient pathways to be established. Staff can learn from real evidence about the impact of some of their choices across the patient journey and can compare their choices made to those of their peers helping staff training and improving levels of patient care.

In a related development, hospitals are now looking at the widespread digitalisation of their activities. Many hospitals face extreme budgetary pressures and are looking at technology and new digital ways of working as the route to better managing themselves. They are starting with real-time analysis of incoming demand on their services, including the tracking of ambulance dispatches to better prepare for the arrival of emergency cases. They are monitoring bed availability across all Hospital Departments to be able to more quickly admit patients from Accident and Emergency, as well as balance the number of beds needed for elective care, thereby reducing backlogs and freeing up capacity. They are also tracking patient discharges working with community care services to be able to ensure the prompt provision of appropriate follow-up care.

CONCLUSION

This book aimed to provide a concise reference guide for those wanting to define Data Strategy and embark on a journey of data transformation. Drawing on my experience of having seen successful and unsuccessful Data Strategy delivery, I set out to write a book that would provide the reader with the necessary help to get their Data Strategy started in the right way and help them cut through the vested interests of different stakeholder groups to ensure that their Data Strategy is implemented successfully.

It was written for those familiar enough with the world of data to realise that there are better ways and worse ways to embark on Data Strategy. Whether the reader is responsible for the Data Strategy, such as a Chief Data Officer, or somebody working in one of the many data domains, the purpose of this book was to share a robust framework of topics to be addressed in the formulation and delivery of an organisation's Data Strategy.

The Data Strategy Framework described in Figure 1, provides a tried and tested approach to reviewing all the important perspectives needed for successful Data Strategy definition and implementation. It concisely describes the key elements that need to be addressed when developing a Data Strategy Roadmap, establishing the Business Case for initiatives, developing the Target Operating Model for delivery, identifying the Stakeholders impacted and creating the related necessary Communications Plan for success. These same elements are also used when considering an organisation's Data Maturity Assessment and the Business Impact Analysis needed for data to be used and governed correctly.

Throughout this book, the importance of *Selling the Value* of an organisation's Data Strategy has been emphasised. Without a continued focus on *Selling the Value* it is all too easy, for example, to get carried away by exciting new technologies, caught-up in the complexities of managing delivery teams, risk developing processes for the sake of process and becoming bogged-down in never-ending battles with data quality. Instead, by focusing on *Selling the Value* of an organisation's

Data Strategy, it reminds those working with data to understand what their objective is: to support the organisation in its mission through the use of data and its data related activities.

A Data Strategy that supports the organisation in its mission by efficiently and effectively using data and conducting data related activities, is one that will be supported by the organisation's Senior Leadership Team and is also one that all people in the organisation can understand the importance of. From bitter experience, a Data Strategy that has not achieved buy-in from senior stakeholders and the wider organisation is one that is unlikely to deliver. Initiatives will become stuck, resources will get frozen, other priorities will be allowed to take precedence and the Data Strategy will under-deliver. In many ways, it is better that Data Strategy activities that are not aligned to or that do not deliver enough value to the organisation, should await their turn for when the organisation is ready to see their worth.

This is a conscious choice to focus on priorities and the priorities are defined as those that deliver greatest value to the organisation. It does not mean that only big initiatives will achieve the grade, but it does mean that all initiatives within the Data Strategy need to have a compelling reason for their inclusion. It probably also means that there is a long list of candidate initiatives, but only a smaller list of actual signed-off and included initiatives in the Data Strategy. The availability of resources is limited in all organisations and so not everything can be implemented in one go and new priorities will come along to change the make-up of the list.

On too many occasions, discussions around technology get in the way of adequate Data Strategy definition. Business Users, Developers, Architects and probably all of us at times, can all too easily get lost in the thrall of exciting new technological developments and desirable new features. This is not to say these are not important, on the contrary, they have been developed for a reason: but how they will contribute to the delivery of value is the important question. All new technology needs to be considered in terms of how it will support the delivery of value better than other choices of technology available. The business case for a data related initiative needs to show that the returns gained from using the new technology are greater than sticking with existing tooling or other alternative choices. The Data Strategy should be about the value you get from a data related initiative not the technology you happen to be using in delivering this initiative.

Far too often tensions around the need to manage people in different ways comes to the fore in Data Strategy discussions. For example, existing managers want larger teams, preferences for localised versus centralised delivery models come and go like the tides and the desired capability gains can be slower to achieve than people hope. All such issues are important and need to be addressed, however how they are addressed is the important point.

A new team structure, a new approach to delivery and new investments in people skills are all important, but how these new approaches support the delivery of value over and above existing approaches is key. All new people related structures and capabilities need to deliver greater value than alternative choices. A Data Strategy should be about the value you generate from a data related initiative and how you are optimally deploying your internal human resources and support partners to enable its efficient and effective delivery. And, the development of new organisational structures, new training and new capabilities should only be pursued once the Data Strategy is defined, so that the ways of working are developed to support the value to be generated.

Poor quality data, badly managed datasets, missing standards and policies, alongside all manner of data governance concerns, all too often impact Data Strategy. All of these cause re-work and the amount of re-work needed in many data related initiatives is often far too large. The costs of these remedial activities need to be factored into the Data Strategy and taken into account when calculating the value that any data related initiative will bring. Governance of all data and data related activities must not be ignored, and certainly the initiatives within an organisation's Data Strategy Roadmap will need governance to ensure their successful delivery. The deployment of standards, development of policies and incubation of an effective data etiquette all will provide economies over time in the delivery of governance practices.

Likewise, data related processes need to be periodically reviewed to ensure they are working as optimally as possible. New data related processes should be developed when they are necessary and the advantages of these new processes should be clearly visible. Ways of working should primarily be developed in conjunction with the delivery of the Data Strategy and the cost-benefit analysis around these new processes should be factored into the value delivered by an initiative.

This continued focus on *Selling the Value* enables stakeholders to have confidence that the related efforts will be paid back in the anticipated benefits and returns. It means that the Data Strategy which is aligned to the organisation's Strategy will support and deliver benefits to the organisation's Mission and Purpose. It should therefore remove any issues that any Data Strategy initiative is not needed or necessary. It should likewise provide a compelling reason so that the resources needed for the successful delivery of the Data Strategy are made available. Through tracking delivery, it should also be possible to demonstrate the on-going value that these Data Strategy initiatives bring.

By focusing on *Selling the Value*, an organisation is better equipped to navigate the plethora of choices available in today's data rich and increasingly digital world. A mindset that thinks about the choices from a benefits gained perspective is more likely to secure success and not get distracted by unnecessary activities or initiatives. And, by delivering the Data Strategy in a systematic and incremental manner, it will help establish robust foundations on which subsequent developments can be built. In this way, budgets are better managed, resources are used to better effect and the Data Strategy receives the best chances for long-term success.

So many exciting things are happening today with data, it's time for all organisations to embrace the opportunities available from using data to deliver value. Having a Data Strategy in place and *Selling the Value* is the way to achieve success.

ABOUT THE AUTHOR

Dr. Doug McConchie is an author, advisor and coach specialising in how best to transform data into business insights, data driven solutions and value. He works within the IoT, Business Intelligence, Analytics and Performance Management community. He helps organisations better acquire, manage, measure, report and analyse their data, leveraging insights to improve their performance. And, his expertise is relied on to develop Data Strategy and secure benefits for his clients' data related transformational activities.

His cutting-edge work with well-known businesses and public sector institutions equips him with a wealth of experience. He has advised and worked internationally with some of the world's best-known organisations including: BP, Credit Agricole, Deutsche Telecom, ExxonMobil, Gartner, Hitachi, Mars, Ministry of Defence, NHS, RBS, RSA, SAB Miller, Sony, and Shell, among many others.

With a doctorate in Strategy his approach guides organisations with the necessary rigour to de-risk data initiatives and help achieve success. He brings to his engagements experience about the practicalities of making solutions work at the operational level and developing new ways of harnessing data for commercial advantage.

Printed in Great Britain
by Amazon